HEALING
MYSELF

HEALING MYSELF

A Hero's Primer for
Recovery from Tragedy

GARI CARTER

HAMPTONROADS
PUBLISHING COMPANY, INC.

Cover Photo by Dr. Steven E. Heyman

The following quotations in the text are
with permission of each publisher:

Inayat Kahn, as included in *Complete Sayings*, ©1978, Omega
Publications, New Lebanon, NY 12125

Dorothy Maclean, *To Hear the Angels Sing: An Odyssey of Co-Creation
with the Devic Kingdom*, ©1990, Lindisfarne Press, Hudson, NY
12534

Dag Hammarskjold, *Markings*, ©1964, Alfred A. Knopf, Inc., New
York, NY 10022

Richard Bach, *Illusions*, ©1977, Dell Publishing, New York, NY
10103

Louise L. Hay, *You Can Heal Your Life*, ©1984, Hay House, Carson,
CA 90749

For information write:

Hampton Roads Publishing Company, Inc.
891 Norfolk Square
Norfolk, VA 23502

Or call: (804)459-2453
FAX: (804)455-8907

If you are unable to order this book from your local
bookseller, you may order directly from the publisher.
Quantity discounts for organizations are available.
Call 1-800-766-8009, toll-free.

ISBN 1-878901-75-3

Printed on acid-free paper in the United States of America

In gratitude
To my mother,
who raised me twice with
unending support and love;
To Dr. Milton T. Edgerton,
who patiently sculpted my second face;
To Robert Monroe,
who gave me the grace
of peace and courage;
and
in deepest appreciation
to all my supportive network
who taught me endurance
with love, harmony,
and beauty over the years.

Foreword

Occasionally along the convoluted trail of life, we hear a story of exceptional and persistent courage so great that one thinks and hopes: "This ought to be written down. Others can be helped if they only knew of it."

Not one in a hundred ever gets into print. *Healing Myself* is one such story that beat the odds. Gari Carter's candid account of the cataclysmic accident that destroyed her face and transformed her life forever is certainly one for the books—and so it is! For those who need it, here is fresh testimony as to the strength of the human spirit that can bring hope to those in the midst of tragedy. If you don't need such help now, it is a book to have and to hold until you do—because you probably will.

Among the many injuries suffered by Gari in her auto accident was the destruction of almost her entire face. From this point of devastation came the slow and painful evolution of surgeries to restore her to what she once was—and the realization that she could never be again the Gari of the past, but someone new, different and greater.

We at the Institute were privileged to play a small part in Gari's change through her use of our restorative audio tapes during some of her operations. In Gari's case, we were permitted to videotape one of her latest trips to the operating room, including interviews before and after surgery. It is a fascinating document that attests again to the incredible power of human mind consciousness.

Which of course, is the theme of *Healing Myself.* All of us have such power, and Gari shows us a profound application of it. Maybe we can use it too when and if we need it.

Robert Monroe

Chapter 1

I worried when it began to snow. Being an optimist, I thought it would stop. A voice kept saying, "Gari Carter, return home." My son and I discussed turning around and going home. We decided to drive another five minutes to see if the snow became fiercer. That decision drastically changed our lives. I have often wondered how my life would be if I had listened to my intuition.

We were on our way from Virginia to a gift show in Baltimore to select new spring items for my shop in February 1982. I had opened a successful clothing and gift shop five years earlier, drawing on my experience modeling since I was a teenager, and had made a profit from the first year on. I loved the shop, but it was like a new baby, always on my mind and creating tremendous hard work. I felt that it was part of the reason my husband and I had gone our separate ways after twenty years of marriage. Our daughter Emily had just chosen to live with him, which devastated me. She was thirteen, a Page in the Virginia Legislature that year and home only on weekends. It was hard for me to realize that I was no longer the Perfect Mother. At least I still had our son—Thomas was eleven and immersed in Cub Scouts, soccer, matchbox cars, and friends. Tom was excited about traveling with me for the weekend to visit family and help me find new treats for the shop.

While I drove along, I thought about my compartments of family relationships. I remembered the distance I had always felt between my mother and myself. I wondered again why she always had to tell me my lipstick was wrong or my slip was showing. My father was not as critical of me while he was still alive. Other mothers did not seem as demanding as mine. Today, I thought, she would approve of me. I was tall, slim and proud of my large brown eyes and shiny shoulder-length chestnut hair. I had lost twenty pounds due to worry about my recent family problems. I wore the one pair of slacks which still fit, with a shirt, blazer and warm down-filled coat to protect me from the snow. Even though I had lost a husband and a child, I was determined to continue to make my shop a success and life happy for my remaining child and myself. Somehow, I would be enabled to create love and meaning in my life.

I realized that I must stop musing and pay closer attention to the icy road. We were on a narrow two-lane country road in Virginia on our way to the main highway. There were no houses in that area—just woods called The Wilderness, where many died in a Civil War battle. Large fluffy snowflakes rushed toward my misted car windows. My windshield wipers had increased trouble keeping a space open. I pressed forward against my seat belt to see through the foggy tunnel of trees. I knew my own driving was good in the snow (I had lots of practice growing up in Connecticut) but was never sure of other drivers. I considered returning home, but again overruled my inner voice. The shop needed new gifts to fill in until my next buying trip to New York. Also, Tom and I had agreed to try driving five more minutes. The new steel-studded snow tires on my Datsun gave me confidence, even when I felt the car starting to slip at times. I loved my cheerful little yellow car with my shop logo on each side. It was a constant advertisement, just as I was, by always wearing the shop's latest styles.

We had almost driven our five-minute limit. Suddenly, a huge shape loomed in my window. A station wagon lost control on a curve. It rapidly veered straight at us in our lane. The white drifts of snow were closing in even faster. We were encapsulated in silent terror.

There was a guardrail on my right; I could not pull off the road to get out of the way. All I could think was, "My son has to be all right. I do not care about myself. Tom must not be hurt. Please keep him safe." I pulled my wheel sharply to the left. Perhaps I could escape to the other side of the road. We were traveling at only thirty miles per hour. My engine did not have the pickup to make it into the other lane in time. The station wagon hit us head-on. My tiny car was pancaked. Intense noises stabbed my ears. Words revolved in my mind, coupled with unbearable metallic clashes. I could not draw any breath to scream, "Oh no, no, no! This is *not* happening to us! Is this how I and my son are going to die?"

Much later, I learned the sequence of events which followed in real life. I was intensely enveloped in a near-death experience at the time. I have snatches of memory. We whipped around and around, faster than any demonic amusement ride. When we stopped turning, Tom ripped off the cloth trash bag which had flown onto his face. It had protected him from broken glass. He wiggled his fingers and toes. He realized that he was all right. The major impact had been on my side of the car. Unbuckling his seat belt, he jumped out, breaking his door as he slammed it. He ran around to my side of the car to open my door and help me. Suddenly, with a shock, he realized that his mother was not breathing. My face was one big open gory hole, smashed between the steering wheel and headrest. My body was trapped in the car by twisted metal. Broken glass was everywhere. The engine was jammed into my legs. He frantically remembered the first steps in CPR he had studied in Cub Scouts the week before. He shook me, saying "Please, please." Luckily, I started gasping through the ugly bloody hole, which had been my mouth and nose. He felt helpless, since he could not move or drag me out of the car. He desperately screamed for help.

Later, when I asked him how he could have started

me breathing when I looked horrifying, he said, "You don't think, when it is someone you care about. You just do what you have to." I am sure I could not have done the same at his young age. I feel incredibly lucky to have had such a mature child, one who saved his mother's life. The memory of his courage still brings tears of love and gratitude to my eyes, to think of what he gave me—my second chance to live.

A lady who lived in a trailer nearby was letting her cat outside and saw and heard the crash. She sent her husband out in the deep snow to help, as she dialed 911 to alert the Rescue Squad. The man brought a blanket to shield me from the snow and took Tom into their trailer to dry off and warm up. Tom later said he was terrified that I would die out there all alone in the car and he would be left without a mother. He wanted to go back out and help in some way but, being a child, was kept inside. The girls from the car who hit us were also brought into the trailer. They all had minor injuries, despite not wearing seat belts, as they were in a big heavy American car.

I was trapped alone in the squashed car, covered by the mercifully thick blanket. My partial face was pricked by the sharp cold wind and hissing snow, since all the windows were gone. My normally active mind felt simply there, in limbo. I did not worry until I felt heat and realized that my car engine was on fire. Incredibly, a passing driver saw the accident, recognized my car, and stopped. He immediately noticed the flames flickering under the smashed hood. He threw handfuls of snow on the fire to put it out. He ripped the bent hood apart and disconnected everything he could reach in the engine. He explained what he was doing, to reassure me. I could not see or smell the fire. I had a strong sense that all was being taken care of and felt very peaceful. The passerby stayed with me until the Rescue Squad arrived and then quietly left. Several months later, I found out who he was and thanked him for saving my life.

Several Rescue Squads were alerted. The one from

my town was fifteen miles away, so it arrived first and attended to me as the most urgent injury. Another town's Rescue Squad took the four college students from the other car to the Fredericksburg Hospital. Tom was kept in the trailer to ride with me to the University of Virginia Hospital in Charlottesville. Diplomatically, accident victims and families are separated this way by emergency crews.

Someone else driving by read the logo on my car and called the shop to alert them about the accident. Mary and Louise, the manager and assistant, were working that day. Mary took the call. She had just said goodbye to me about thirty minutes earlier, after we finished compiling the list of gifts I needed to find at the show. At first, she thought the call was a prankster. She could not believe what she was hearing. She mechanically thanked the caller, sat down in shock, and told Louise. They decided that Louise should close up the store and go home, before the snow became worse. Mary notified my former husband and called her husband Bob, who was on the Rescue Squad. Bob and Mary drove out to the accident; Mary went directly into the trailer to comfort Tom. He was reassured to see a familiar face and relieved to learn that the Rescue Squad was getting me out of the car. Bob went to assist the other squad members in the snow.

The volunteer Rescue Squad from my tiny town arrived with the "Jaws of Life," which they had only recently been able to afford to buy. The team set to work right away. The first and only trained female squad member climbed into the passenger seat and put her arm comfortingly around my shoulder. She spoke soothingly to me. "Trust me. Everything will be all right. Don't worry. I won't leave you alone." She then explained what was happening. The big machine began to tear the car apart. I remember sensing the steering wheel, which was inches away from my cut eyes, begin to jerk away from my face. I shook with terror, as I heard the first angry screeches from the protesting car. I remembered the crash noises. The Squad member patted my shoulder and reassured me. She helped me remain calm as the car ripped open with huge terrifying metallic crunching noises. I knew they were trained to be careful. They had to pull the metal apart to avoid mangling my right leg, which was three-quarters severed by the engine. Being in shock, I felt no pain.

When the mutilated car was finally open enough to get me out, the Rescue Squad lady slipped away. Suddenly, I felt millions of hands and arms gently coming from everywhere and carefully floating me out and away. I was terrified that my body would start hurting. Surprisingly, I was encompassed by a warm, secure, comforting cloud, despite the cold and snow. I wondered if this were what angels' hands felt like when they touched you and if I were on my way to Heaven. I was apprehensive that my son was not all right, because I could not see. My eyes were cut from the broken glass. My contact lenses were later found imbedded in my sheepskin car seat covers.

Meanwhile, my daughter Emily and her father arrived. Emily said later that he told her to wait by the car, to protect her from seeing me. He left her standing alone in the wet, freezing snow. He rushed over to see if he could help the other men. She shivered, cold and alone as she cried for her mother, afraid to move. There was a backup of cars in both directions as far as she could see. The State Police and Rescue Squad were trying to clear the way. Her father finally returned to her just as the doors slammed shut on the Rescue Squad ambulance and Tom and I were rushed away. She asked her father, "Why can't I see Mummy?" He told her that I did not have a face anymore, as they walked over to my car. She cried as she saw my blood everywhere—on the car dashboard, seats, floor and doors. The sawed-off steering wheel was resting on the crumpled hood, covered with bloody mounds of snow glimmering with shards of broken glass.

Bob had returned to the trailer to take Tom to the van for the drive to the hospital. Mary ran alongside them and exclaimed, "I must tell Gari that Tom is unhurt before they leave."

Bob shook his head, lifted Tom into the front seat, shut the door and then quietly said, "I don't think she's going to make it. She has no face left."

Mary hysterically insisted, "I don't care! If I tell her, she will believe me. I need to do this for her. I know how I would feel if my child were with me in an accident." She entered the back of the van and was jolted, as she saw the hole where my face had been. She swallowed and managed to say in a calm voice, "Gari, don't worry about Tom. He was not hurt. He is riding in the front seat with you to the hospital. Everything will be all right when you get to a doctor. The shop is fine. Louise and I will take care of it. Don't worry about anything." Sadly, I was not conscious of her kind effort. She told me later that I kept restlessly reaching for her hand. She was not sure that I was aware of what she said, or that she had made any difference. As my friend, she had to try. She quickly jumped out of the van, overwhelmed with grief, as the siren was activated and we moved into the snowstorm.

As my stretcher lurched from the fast driving, I suddenly felt and heard a ripping and cutting on my legs. The squad members were slicing up the sides of my slacks. I silently despaired, "Oh no! This is the only pair I have that fit me!" Next I felt more bursts of cold, as they cut up the arms of my down coat, blazer and shirt. I realized that even if I were able to speak, it would not have done any good. They had to act quickly. I already missed my warm clothes. I laughed to myself as I remembered my mother always saying to wear nice clean underwear, in case I were in an accident. Now I was in one and I did have on the proper undies, but it did not matter. No one looked at its niceness, but just cut it up. So much for obeying motherly advice!

Tom and I were rushed to the University of Virginia Medical Center Hospital in Charlottesville. Luckily, in the Plastic Surgery Department, there is a Craniofacial Clinic — one of five in the country — where doctors work on the underlying bones, as well as the face, in reconstruction. I knew nothing of this specialty beforehand and was to learn later how kind and thoughtful they were in dealing with all aspects of a deformity. Tom was separated from me as the Rescue Squad dashed us inside the Emergency Room. I still agonized that my son was hurt or dead. I would not believe anyone until I could see for myself. I no longer felt serene and secure with all the agitation, commotion, bright lights and loud noises. A horde of people burst around me asking rapid, sharp questions. Orthopedics and Craniofacial Plastic Surgery were called. My stretcher was wheeled into the Operating Room, where the surgeons began repairing me quickly, as my mind floated away. They later joked that they each had their own territories of my body — Orthopedics from the hips down and Plastics from the neck up.

First, a tracheotomy incision was made into my throat and a tracheostomy tube inserted, so that my breathing could be controlled and the doctors could manage anaesthesia without my having a nose or mouth. Next, the orthopedic surgeons repaired my severed leg, reattaching all the numerous minute muscles, nerves and ligaments and salvaging what they could of my shattered patella or kneecap. They set the broken bones and put gauze dressings and splints on them. The leg lacerations were sutured or sewn up to heal; casts were put on at a later date. Meanwhile, the plastic surgeons were stitching the layers of my face back together. As the hole reached from my neck to my eyes, they began at the deepest part under the eyes, working down and out. I later learned, to my frustration, that repairing a face is like constructing a house. You have to have a firm foundation inside before you can start what is seen outside. At this point, the important thing was to close up all wounds as fast as possible so that I would survive. Later, they would be able to operate to repair and restructure the bones. By then, I had lost a good deal of blood and there was concern about saving my life.

Meanwhile, Tom was judged unhurt by the doctors in the Emergency Room. Emily and her father arrived as he was released. The two children sat alone for a long time in the waiting room. Emily noticed that Tom's hair was full of blood, like the car. She looked down and was angry that he had a pair of patterned shoelaces in his shoes that she had wanted for herself from my shop. Tom worried that the zipper tab of his new ski jacket was bent from the accident. He zipped it up and down. The zipper still worked, but it looked broken. He would remember the accident every time he zipped it from then on. Whenever the anxious children asked about me, they were told that I was still in surgery. They wanted my surgery to hurry up, so they could leave.

Since we lived in a small town, the story traveled like the wind. People rallied to help. My friend Blair appeared at the hospital to take both children to spend the night with her. Tom later told me that he had a terrible time sleeping. Every time he closed his eyes, he saw the huge car coming right at us with no way to escape. The same vision reappeared each time he daydreamed in school for several years. The next morning when he and Emily awoke, they found one of my teeth, which had been caught in his hair, resting on his pillow. Adult teeth have very long roots—totally unlike those they had saved for the tooth fairy. The tooth brought back all their dreadful memories and they cried together, wondering how I was. Blair saved the tooth in a Bloomingdale's jewelry box and brought it to me later in the hospital, in case I needed it to help in making new teeth. I still have it as a reminder of what I once was, tucked away at the back of my nightgown drawer.

After many hours of surgery, I was taken to the

nearby Recovery Room. This is a bright open room with strong lights. Patients are on stretchers inside curtained cubicles, monitored by nurses, as they slowly regain consciousness after surgery. When all vital signs are normal, patients are returned to their rooms.

Meanwhile, my former husband began calling my family, as he waited at the hospital until I was out of surgery. He first called my stepmother, with whom Tom and I were to spend the weekend, to explain our absence. My mother was reached in Florida on vacation. She was unable to get a flight to Virginia right away and felt frantic that I might not live until she arrived. The children's godmother offered to keep my dog. She drove down the next day in the snow from Washington and thoughtfully cleaned out my refrigerator as well. Later, I felt overwhelmed with gratitude as I learned of all the kind friends and relatives who did unasked favors for me during the crisis.

Chapter 2

I have fleeting impressions of my time in limbo. When one is in a coma, the sense of hearing is sometimes still there. I could not see; my eyes were stitched up. I could not talk because the tracheostomy controlled my shallow breathing. Most of my face was sewn up to heal. I could not taste anything without a mouth to eat—all my nourishment came from intravenous feeding. I could not smell without a nose. I could touch only with my right hand, as all the rest of my body was either tied or weighted down. I did not want to move, due to the incredible stabs of pain. There was a huge totality of agony in every particle of my body. I simply existed inside my pain-filled shell. It was like a symphony—suddenly different unimaginable spots would be featured, catching me off guard with new pain which overrode the background hurts. My existence flowed in pain without ceasing. I had no idea where I was or what had happened to me. I was in a new, unknown, incongruous world populated with strangers, in which I had lost all memory of who I formerly was. I did not know where I lived. Did I have a family? I really did not care. I just wanted the intense, enveloping pain to stop.

When I floated into semi-alertness, I would hear flashes of loud conversations of foreign medical language and not understand how they related to me. Some people would talk as if I were not able to hear them. Others talked as if I could answer, though there was no chance. Some had gentle, soft touches and were thoughtful in the way they did whatever they had to do to me. Others jerked and pummeled me like a huge truck mashing me, immersing me in more incredible, overwhelming hurts. There were noises of bells ringing, rattling carts, wheelchairs rolling, shuffling people walking, fast purposeful people walking in squishy rubber-soled shoes—a strange assortment of noises to identify. I was attached to the real world only with my ears. I felt maimed and lost without my other senses. All these fleeting impressions did not add up to anything; I felt as if I were in a strange prison of insistent torturous pain. I did not care enough to find out where I was or who I was or why I was there, before floating back into merciful unconsciousness.

The first awareness came when I was visited by a friend after my eye bandages were removed. Visitors were allowed for only ten minutes, but Alice was determined to see me. She cheerfully said, "Hello," as she walked into the room. Instantly, with that one word, I knew who I was and who she was and what had happened to me and why she was there. She had been in a severe car accident when she was eighteen. It took her many months to heal and that was why she had come to visit me. I could not see her. I could not answer her without my mouth. My left arm was tied down with a nest of intravenous tubes, so I lifted my one free hand and waved to show I was still a part of the living world. She asked, "Could you manage to write with a pad and pencil?" I made a little wave again and she went out to the nurses' station and found some. She put the pad gently on my stomach and the pencil in my right hand and guided me to the paper. The first joyful words I laboriously wrote were "Thank you!" I could remember to write without looking, so I must be all right after all! I was excited and happy to be able to communicate again—what a wonderful gift from a thoughtful friend! I felt as if I were Helen Keller suddenly able to communicate with the world. The pain could not be as unbearable and everything would have to be all right with control of my mind and identity returned to me.

Next, my worried mother and stepfather arrived from Florida. My mother told me later that she was exhausted by the time she finally got to see me. When she arrived at the hospital, the head nurse on the floor refused to allow her in my room, as visiting hours were over. The nurse told her to talk to the general doctor in charge of my case first. Mum went to find him and was horrified as he described my injuries. All she wanted to do was see me and reassure herself that I was still alive. When she got out of the doctor's office, she felt faint. She leaned against the wall of the hallway, wishing for someone to rescue her. The resident doctor assigned to me noticed her and asked if he could help. By then, my mother was practically in tears and said, "All I want to do is see my daughter." Dr. Philip Lambruschi took her gently by the arm and marched her right by the head nurse into my room. He told Mum to call him if she needed any help in the future.

Mum was appalled by the shapeless bandaged blob, woven by tubes into many machines, which was supposed to be her pretty daughter. She controlled her grief. She walked to the side of my bed and leaned over with her face close to mine. She hoped I could see her as she said, "I'm here, Darling, and I'll make sure you have the best possible care—you don't have to worry—your Mum is not going to leave you." I heard her through my fog of pain and knew then that everything would be all right, or my protective mother would take on the world to make sure it was. What a gift to have a strong loving mother now! She kissed her finger and hesitantly put it on my swollen forehead, afraid to touch any part of what had been my face. She was determined not to show her distress, to give me confidence, since she felt I would need an abundance to survive and recover.

I was drifting in and out of pain and consciousness then and could never get comfortable. I moved as little as possible to prevent the hard mattress pummeling me. I did not want any more than the minimum hurts. My biggest fear was the tracheostomy clogging up. The first time it happened, I panicked that I was to die then and there. Luckily, my mother was with me. She darted, screaming at the nurses' station, "My daughter is not breathing and needs help immediately!" A busy nurse ran in and started the ventilator. The first breath is too tiny for what is needed, but feels like cool breezes of beauty inside the lungs. One wants more and more after struggling and getting no air. Each time this happened, the nurses seemed unconcerned. It was my life at stake, not theirs. To prevent the tube clogging, the nurses periodically had to insert saline drops to make me cough, to dislodge mucus and crusts in the lower respiratory tract. Then the tube was aspirated or suctioned out. Both the coughing and aspirating were painful and frightening to me. I dreaded each process.

A "trach" feels terrifying. A wide tracheostomy tube was taped into a hole in my throat and secured with a tie around my neck. The other end of the tube was attached to a big ventilator, which does the "breathing." Before, whenever I took a breath, I did it automatically, without thinking, and could make it small or large as I chose. With a "trach," each breath was strenuous work. I could manage only tiny, shallow breaths, no matter how much I tried for a true deep one. Because each breath grabbed up short, I was ready for the next one too soon. It was worse than panting. If you take a deep breath, let it half out and then try to take another big breath, that is similar to the feeling and amount of air one is able to take in with a tracheostomy. I could never relax, but had to use all my energy just to keep breathing. I was always afraid that the next breath would not be there, and sometimes it eluded me. I felt as if I were under water, trying to save my breath to get to the surface, but never able to get the hang of it in time. My mouth seemed useless. I could move my fat tongue, though it felt weird. I thought I remembered how to speak, but could not make any sounds come out. The inside of my mouth felt raw with enormous chasms, empty of teeth, which hurt to explore. I longed for the freedom to breathe and speak, as I had in my first life. I wanted everything to hurry up and be the way it had been. I still had no intimations that I was starting a new and different second life.

After a few weeks, my children were allowed to visit me. Their world seemed intensely real and bright, compared to my fog of pain and medicine. I felt as if I were in a darkened room in which the shades had been suddenly raised, as Tom's face floated near mine. I was overwhelmingly relieved to see that he truly was uninjured. I longed to cry. Weeping sounds did not emerge, although I could feel my throat tighten and my eyelids prick with uncried tears. The unspeakable horror of what had happened washed through me. I had been filled with dread and guilt since the accident, afraid that he was either badly hurt or dead. I thought that I had killed my son and that no one would tell me the truth. I wrote on my pad, "I am thrilled to see you are all right!" Tom gave me a gentle bear hug as best he could, saying "Grr" as he had since he was tiny. He told me he was fine. He laughed as he saw how I wrote words on top of words on my pad, which I could not see. He said, "My teachers would never let me write as sloppily in school." He sat by my side and moved the pad as I wrote, so he could read my answers out loud.

My daughter Emily, who still looks like my first face, was horrified speechless when she saw what was left of her mother. She felt that I looked just like a swollen Egyptian mummy—all white and bandaged. My hair was thickly caked with dried blood. She was sure what she saw in the bed was dead. The ugly body inside all those bandages could not be the pretty mother she remembered. She walked in slowly, thinking maybe it would change as she got closer. Surely her real mother would be in the hospital bed, instead of the deformity she saw. She stopped at the foot of my bed and held tightly onto the frame, as her eyes got wider and bigger. My mother caught her just as she started to faint and took her away. They found a nurse to revive her with ammonia. It took several years, until most of the outer damage had been repaired, before she could bear to look at me again. She accepted only her vivid memories of the past, unable to comprehend that her mother would never be the same. Even now, she clings to the memory of my first face whenever she thinks of me. This was my first experience with what some reactions would be to my new disfigured appearance. I had not been allowed to look in a mirror. I simply thought I had a few minor scars and did not understand why people were upset to see me. It was still me inside and I thought they should be able to understand. I would be up and racing down the halls in a few days anyway. I was invincible.

By then, I had learned to use my other senses slightly. My eyes were open, but, being very nearsighted, I saw only impressions beyond my immediate surroundings. When I tried squinting to see better, everything doubled, so I preferred the haze. Even tiny movements stabbed me, so I planned each move to outwit my enemy pain. I was very careful to lie as quietly as possible. Moving required energy I did not have. Slow, careful, thoughtful movements made it easier to breathe with the constant, permeating pain, just as I had learned years ago with Lamaze preparations for childbirth. My main concern was to endure as long as I could, not knowing when the pain would end. I relished whatever relief from pain I got. I could touch and feel a restricted area with my right hand, but tasting and smelling were out of my realm of abilities. With my ears, I could tell from the footsteps whether the person entering my room was male or female by the weight and slap of the stride on the floor. Usually, nurses and doctors sounded more purposeful and busy than visitors; plus, with rubber-soled shoes, they were quieter. Visitors would pause hesitantly in front of my door to check the name and then enter. Some were excessively cheerful, trying to follow the unspoken rule of "not noticing." Others recoiled and gasped at the shock of my missing face, as they tried to mask the sound and cover up quickly. No one paid attention to my leg injuries under the sheet. All attention was directed to my lost face, which could not be hidden by clothing or bedding.

One day, my attorney came to visit and followed the latter pattern. He managed to say "Hi, Gari" in a semi-normal voice but choked and lost control as he said his name. He sat down on the window sill by my bed, trying not to cry at the sight of what was left of me. When he could talk again, he asked, "Is there anything I can do for you?"

I grabbed my pen and wrote, "You better represent me in this accident or else!"

He started laughing and said, "I'm glad to know there is still a tiger inside there. Don't worry, I will take care of everything legal for you." His remark gave me courage from then on that I could spend my energy healing and let others organize my life. I had lost, in an instant, all mature control over my life, for which every child strives. When I was discouraged from fear or pain, I would take heart and renewed courage from his remark about the tiger inside me and smile to myself.

Many reactions made me wonder if people thought they were dealing with a vegetable just because I looked so smushed. People really do judge others by their looks. I began to realize I would not be able to be out in public for a while. I longed to blend into a crowd without stares. I had lost a husband, a child, a face, and heaven knows what else in my legs. Everything I had valued before was stripped from me. How could I build a new life from the few narrow shreds left? Every time I allowed myself to think realistically about my future, I was crushed by the hopelessness of it all. I had worked hard all my life to become independent, create a family and help others. Now I was reduced to beginning again as an ugly, deformed cripple, on a quest for meaning in a totally changed life. What had I done to deserve this? How could I ever dare to hope for the joy and magic of a normal life in the future?

A wonderful Episcopal minister, Mr. Clark, noticed my name on the patient roster and brought his wife in to see me. We had many ties; he had grown up with my father, I had been in the same class as their daughter in college, and he had been the rector of my church on the Eastern Shore of Virginia, when my son was born. Tom developed septicemia (blood poisoning) at birth, which necessitated us staying three long, scary weeks in the tiny local hospital. Each day, Mr. Clark came to visit and pray with me. I realized how serious Tom's condition was when I found that Mr. Clark had left his phone number at the nurses' station. He told them to call any time of the day or night if Tom became more critical. Now, when I was in need, he had just retired to Charlottesville. He told me, "We will be here every day for you, Gari. You know you are in our prayers for a full and speedy recovery. How wonderful it is that Tom gave you life, as you gave it to him! Have the nurses call us any time you need us." My eyes shone with tears at his wonderful compassion and understanding. How could I not survive and emerge as a valuable new self, with such thoughtful, concerned people surrounding me? The Clarks were true to their word and kept in constant touch with many visits in the years to come.

Chapter 3

Once I remembered my shop, I realized that I was lucky to have no worries due to my capable manager, Mary, and my terrific employees. The summer before, I had driven my children on a three-month trip around the United States, calling in frequently to answer questions and help make decisions. Mary had already known how to run everything, but had never done it alone. She gained the confidence necessary that summer. The assistant manager, Louise, stepped right in whenever Mary was gone. The two of them managed smoothly with the other employees, salesmen, customers and the daily running of the business. By the end of the summer, I seldom needed to call.

Neither Mary nor Louise had been among my original employees. When I opened the shop, I hired six part-time employees of different ages and interests to attract diverse groups of customers to the store. We quickly became good friends. Mary's daughter, Susan, was my teenaged employee and wonderful with customers — always cheerful, helpful and available. One day, I had to put on a fashion show and everyone else was either sick or busy at the last minute. I did not want to close the shop and lock the door while I was narrating the show. Susan was modeling for me that day and suggested her mother could fill in. I was not thrilled with the idea, since I had not met her. She had no clothing store experience, but, desperate to stay open, I agreed. Mary arrived and I asked her if she knew how to run a cash register. When she said yes, I smiled and said "Fine" and raced out the door with all the outfits for the show, leaving her alone with no instructions. We later laughed many times together about it, as she turned out to be a terrific employee.

Louise arrived after Mary. I had thought for a long time that she would be a wonderful addition to our group, but was afraid to ask her, as I did not think she would be interested. When I finally found the courage to ask, she was not sure she wanted to work but decided to give it a try for a while, since everyone had such fun in my shop. The "little while" never ended and was another lucky break for me and my shop.

After a few weeks of slipping into the real world, I longed to have my glasses to see again. When my mother brought them in and put them on me, they slid down my face, leaving a trail of hurt. Mum was very inventive and thought of ways to pad them with gauze or tape them to my forehead, but they still fell off. She took them to the optician, who ground off the nosepieces and padded the center of the frame. He tightened the earpieces, so that my ears would bear the weight. When my mother brought them back and I could keep them on my non-face, it was a shock to see clearly. I felt a stabbing pain like a headache behind my eyes. I was not sure I really wanted to see the world precisely again. I had managed so far in my nearsighted impressionistic haze. My new world felt as if I were going into a dark movie theatre, groping for a seat and then suddenly being blinded with excessively sharp and luridly colored images. I decided to change to the real world in slow stages. I was glad to see friendly people and lovely flowers clearly, but not my myriad of machines to which I was tethered or the utilitarian hospital room.

The pain was constant, drenching my body. As every move started new pain radiations, I was careful to stay as immobile as possible. Everything imaginable exhausted me. I needed all my strength to cope with the pain. If I moved in slow motion, the new pain was softer and easier to fit in with the constant ones. I dreaded anyone touching or moving me, as they could never do it as gently as I did myself; but no one ever wanted to wait for me to move myself. Once I was aware of time, I realized that each moment of pain lasts forever. I wanted the clock to run faster and delete my agony. When I forced myself to think positively, I knew the pain had to end soon. I could not wait to eat from a spoon or drink from a cup or take my first step or skip or dance or do yoga or ski. I had all the wonders of my former life to anticipate. I did not know then that I would have to learn, as if I were a baby, all the skills I used to know, but in new and different ways.

The next step in recovery was to sit in a chair. An aide came to get me and my web of IV's and tracheostomy tubes. Although the ugly, green, vinyl hospital chair was padded, I weighed only eighty-five pounds, and every bone stuck out. Each touch and movement intensified the pain. I was terrified and felt incredibly weak and dizzy in the chair. I hurt inside and out. All I could do was weep silently from the torture. I sat there trying not to feel pain for ten incredibly long minutes, until my worried mother intervened and said, "Put her back in bed; she has had enough."

The aide said, "She is supposed to stay up for a half hour."

My mother insisted, "Put her back in bed or I will do it. You can try longer tomorrow." The aide, in her haste to get me back in bed, hurt me even more. I dissolved into a lump of despair. All I wanted was a shot for pain, so I could fade into needed oblivion. I wondered if life would ever be pain-free or fun again.

The next day was not any better in that hateful green chair. My head throbbed and every bone protested from the unaccustomed pressures of sitting instead of lying. Mum had brought me a Bugs Bunny Magic Slate to replace my pad and pen. I wrote on it, "Please have them put me back in bed. I cannot bear this pain." My mother was concerned because I could not stop crying when sitting up and asked the doctors what else could be giving new pain. After examining me again, they decided to have a dentist check the few remaining teeth, to see if there could be undetected damage.

The next day, my tubes and I were put into a wheelchair and taken to the consulting dentist somewhere in the bowels of the hospital. Mum went along for support and to interpret, in case my Magic Slate was not sufficient. I was terrified, thinking of handling the pain of the dentist on top of my normal amount. The journey seemed to take forever through hallways, down ramps, into and out of several million elevators. Straight rolling was all right, but every doorsill and elevator opening jarred me and showered me with worse pain. I was determined not to cry, despite my head pounding more and more insistently.

I realized that I was spoiled by looks of admiration in public from modeling in my first life. I hated the way most people stared at me now with looks of horror, or a controlled emotionless scrutiny. I felt terribly guilty that I caused their upset expressions. I wanted people to see me as I had been—a human being with feelings like theirs. I found that strangers who did not know me thought with a single glance that they understood me inside and out, pitying me. I longed to return to my cubicle of secrecy on the plastic surgery floor. Luckily, without my glasses, which still hurt to wear more than a few minutes, I could not see anyone clearly. My mother tried to block me from view whenever possible. She fiercely glared at anyone staring at me. A protective mother is certainly valuable!

Finally, we arrived at the dentist's room. The plastic surgeon who would painstakingly construct my new face, Dr. Milton T. Edgerton, Chief of the Craniofacial Clinic, was waiting for a new addition to his staff from Harvard, before beginning work on my reconstruction. Dr. Robert Chuong had a background in dentistry, plastic and craniofacial surgery, which Dr. Edgerton felt was a perfect choice for consultation on my case. Since the new doctor had not arrived, a local dentist was called in to make sure no other damage had been overlooked when my jaw and teeth were patched together in the Emergency Room. With the usual hurts, I was lifted from the wheelchair to the dental chair by the aide. She positioned my tubes and left. The chair seemed incredibly high. I felt a childlike, irrational fear of falling. The seat and armrests sliced into my body. I shifted my exposed bones around to try to find a sliver of comfort, without any success. I realized how much the padding of flesh helps on one's bones. I wished I had some weight back. The chair faced a tiny window up by the ceiling of the damp, cold, subterranean room. I could see a misty fringe of living, pale, green grass and a slivery streak of hazy blue sky. I decided to focus on my pretty view of the real world, instead of my clammy hands and fear of the new unknown additional pain to come. The dentist and his nurse entered and introduced themselves to me and my mother, who hovered beside me. Mum said, "I wonder if she has an abscessed tooth, which is causing her the extra pain when she sits up. Something could have been missed when they treated her in the Emergency Room."

The dentist asked me to open my mouth. It seemed incongruous to open a mouth which could not eat, speak or breathe but still could hurt. As I cautiously obeyed, I unsuccessfully tried not to tense my body. He put his probe into my mouth. He nearly sent me flying through the ceiling with the icy hot bolt of pain from the first tooth he touched. He said, "I am sorry. Let me look with the mirror next." I could not stop my tears. I tried to control myself as my mother gently patted my hand. I had always been afraid of hurting in a dentist's chair; but I never remembered this amount of intense pain. The dentist's second pass into my mouth was much more cautious. It did not hurt, which was a relief.

He said, "You have a shattered tooth there, which has been causing you extra pain. I think you will feel better if we take it out." My mother agreed for me. I held the nurse's hand tightly, as my tears ran down my bandages. The dentist put in horrid, sharp, painful shots of Xylocaine, which I detest. Then Mum and I sat and waited for it to take effect. She stroked my hand as I clenched the armrest.

She reassured me, "That was the worst part, Darling. You really will feel better after the tooth is out." I was exhausted. All I wanted was to be back in my own bed. I needed to sleep and forget this. The dentist and nurse returned. I tried not to look at their terrifying, shiny instruments. I stared at my square of pretty grass and sky. I tried to dream of being outside enjoying them. As the dentist locked onto my tooth, I clutched the nurse's hand. There was a loud crunching noise and a pulling I could feel into the roots of my bloody hair. My mouth suddenly had a huge cold whooshing feeling of air. The tooth broke as the dentist pulled out the largest part.

I thought, "Oh no, I simply can not take any more—this is too much. I want it to be over and be able to lie down and forget it all." The dentist ignored my feelings and went right back into my poor mouth. Luckily, the rest of the tooth came out easily. It was not as bad as I had tensely anticipated. He packed the tooth cavity and gave my mother instructions for taking care of it. He would return to check the wound. I felt numb where the tooth had been. The rest of my body was exhausted and relieved. For once, I was too tired to react to the other hurts. The aide reappeared with the wheelchair and pushed me through the labyrinth of corridors to my room. I was reassured to be back in familiar surroundings, away from prying eyes and voices. On the plastic surgery floor, all the patients were in various stages of reconstruction or change, so I did not look out of place. It was a relief not to be stared at, the way I was in the rest of the hospital. I hoped having the tooth pulled would reduce my pain level. I wondered how I was ever going to gain back the strength to lead a normal life; perhaps it would be easier to survive with dignity when everything did not hurt. All this pain had to end soon. I longed for anyone to give me a final date for hurting. It never happened. I fell asleep gratefully, almost as soon as I was in my bed. My mother guarded the door so that I would not be disturbed.

I was greatly bothered, once I was aware of the real world, by my hair. My two most admired features had always been my shiny chestnut hair and my large brown eyes with their long thick lashes. I hated the idea of losing my former strong points. I could not control the state of my face, but I had a chance to look better if my hair were clean. It was filthy, dirty, and matted with blood and itched incredibly. Frustratingly, I could not even move my good arm close enough to scratch it. The nurses and doctors cleaned my wounds meticulously but ignored my hair. In the beginning, I could not be moved to wash it and later could not bend over a sink. On a slow night, a kind nurse took pity on me and loaded me onto a stretcher and wheeled me into the kitchen. There, she was able to wash my hair in the sink, by easing me as far toward the end of the stretcher as possible and pouring bowls of water over my head. She had to shampoo my hair five times to get out all the dried blood and dirt. Having my hair washed felt like a magical massage, compared to my usual hurts. I wished the water could wash away the accident damage to my body as well. I felt 100 percent better with clean hair and ready to be normal again.

About a month after the accident, Dr. Edgerton felt my face had healed enough for removal of the "trach." Dr. Lambruschi, the resident, zipped the tracheostomy tube out of my throat. He closed the opening with a few stitches. A first, exciting, big live breath filled my lungs with cold relief. I have never before or since had such a special breath. It felt like a symbol of beginning a new life; I had been released from the prison of silence. Dr. Lambruschi cautioned me, "Try not to move your neck too much. We need to keep the edges close together to heal, Gari." No one had to warn me not to move any part of myself—everything hurt!

The pain had lessened slightly in intensity since the tooth had been removed, but there had not been a magical end to pain. Each day, there had been an almost imperceptible improvement, which gave me hope. I wrote on my Magic Slate, "May I really talk now?" and was told that I could. I managed to shape my mouth correctly to say "Thank you!" I was surprised at the sound of my voice and feel of my mouth. I did not sound like me anymore. My first voice had been high and squeaky. This new voice was low, raspy, and soft. I had always wanted to have a well-modulated voice, but never at this physical and emotional expense. My mouth felt full of cotton, as though it were shot with Novocaine. I asked Dr. Lambruschi, "Will my voice be scratchy and deep like this always?"

He said, "It will get smoother as the throat heals and might rise in pitch—time will tell." My throat felt sore from just the two tiny spoken sentences. I resolved to keep my Magic Slate nearby for a while. What a gift to not have to write every communication! So many times we do not realize how we feel about something until we are away from it. I had been apart from speaking for only a month; I had found the loss and inconvenience bearable only because I knew it to be temporary.

After the I.V. tubes were removed, I was introduced to my new way of eating—a Brecht feeder. This is a fat, clear plastic syringe with a foot-long rubber tube attached to the end. The tubes come in varying widths, depending on what one is "eating" and can be cut shorter if needed. In the beginning, I had to leave the tubes long. I put them through my mouth into my throat, so that none of the newly healed areas would get dirty from food. Later, I was able to cut off the length and just squirt food onto my tongue. The narrowest width is used for clear liquids and is not much larger than a huge needle. One gets only tiny trickles of water with it. The wider holes are easier to use. One can squirt more into the mouth with them, so I preferred using wider tubes.

At first, I was given water to practice my new game of eating. It was a challenge to learn to open my deformed mouth enough, without any feeling in the area. The nurses patiently showed me how to feel my face and mouth with one hand, although I did not want to touch myself and hurt more. The skin felt bumpy, yucky, and raw. A mirror would have helped to see what I was doing, but the nurses never mentioned using one. I did not think about it in my determined struggle to succeed. I had to use both hands to fill the syringe—one to steady it and one to pull the plunger. When it was full, I held it in one hand with my index finger on the plunger and guided the tube into my mouth with the other hand. I had to steady the long tubes, as a fireman does holding a hose. The first trickle of liquid beauty down my dry throat was a deeply satisfying source of joy. I felt overwhelmingly weak and clumsy. If I forgot just one tiny motion, I lost control and squirted everything around me, including my face, which had to stay immaculately clean to heal. I wept in frustration each time. It was not only the loss of all the contents of the syringe that upset me, but also the laborious cleaning up again of my face in its raw-hamburger state. I hated to touch myself, afraid I would destroy the shred which was left of me. Every swallow stabbed my throat. I learned to duck my chin to lessen the pain. I was assured that as my throat grew stronger, the pain would retreat.

Now that I could have liquid food, I had a chance to gain some weight, which proved to be just as hard as losing it. While I had been existing on I.V.s, my weight had dropped drastically. All my sharp bones stuck out vulnerably, even if they were not broken. I dreaded having anyone touch me. I truly felt like a concentration camp survivor. My skin was stretched over my gaunt bones in the parts of me I could see. My shoulders, ribs, elbows, wrists, hips, knees and ankles stuck out like jagged Grand Tetons. There was no room for cellulite anywhere—every woman's dream, but not the way anyone would ever want to achieve it!

My yoga and Sufi teacher, Yusuf Quddus Erskine, came to visit regularly. He felt overwhelmed the first day by the modern, medicinal hospital smells and sounds, as well as the sight of me engulfed by bandages and machines. He told me, "I know you will be back in my advanced hatha yoga class, Gari. The doctors said the reason that your spine was not injured was probably due to its flexibility from your yoga exercises over the years. Remember to repeat healing words to yourself and try to use yoga breathing to relax your body from the tension of pain." He reminded me of two of my favorite Sufi quotes from *Gayan, Vadan, Nirtan*, by Hazrat Inayat Kahn. The first states: "What has happened, has happened; What I am going through, I shall rise above; And what will come, I will meet with courage." The second says: "Being alone with one's self is like being with a friend whose company will last forever." They certainly applied to me in my current status. I silently whispered them to myself over and over in the years to come, as I slowly learned who I really was inside that broken body. Yusuf helped me realize that I had drifted along in life before, trying to be whoever people wanted me to be. Now was my time to unwrap within myself the integrity to unfold into the person I was meant to be. I resolved to be true to my own values in the future, by surrounding myself and others with love, harmony and beauty. As Yusuf left he said, "Out of every crisis comes an opportunity. It will be interesting to discover what yours will be. I know you will take good advantage of whatever comes your way." I was reminded of my attorney calling me a tiger. I felt lucky in having perceptive friends to make me aware of what I needed at a time of crisis.

Yusuf turned out to be a wonderful source of help with nutritional information and new foods and additives to try from his health food store. The only way I could get vitamins into my body was in powdered form, mixed into liquid food. He brought me miso soup and soy powder for protein and suggested adding them and other nutritional supplements to my hospital food to build up my weight. The hospital allowed me only clear liquid soups, juices and soupy oatmeal for my experiments in eating; but no one had to know what I did to them in the privacy of my room. Once I was home, I could decide which liquids to drink. My dream was to be able to eat old favorites again—to bite into a crunchy apple or a new ear of corn.

My main job would be to work hard at healing, to be ready for the next reconstructive surgery. Dr. Edgerton's schedule was set five years in advance, so I must be in good health and ready to take the place of a cancellation at any time. I decided to make little goals to achieve, like a mental kindergarten progress chart, to mark each new pound gained by slurping liquid, each additional minute sitting up each day and practicing clear understandable speech without feeling in my mouth. I had an unending list of lessons to learn, in order to enable me to take care of myself again in the future.

Chapter 4

Because of my head injury and all the breaks in my legs, I was often loaded onto a stretcher and taken to x-ray. At first, I was aware only of intensifying pain. Later, as I became more alert, I dreaded the trips. The jerking movement onto the stretcher, the bumpy ride, and the cold, hard x-ray table were new stabs into every inch of my body. I did not feel that any of the aides had special training in lifting or moving injured patients. Perhaps most did not care, just doing a job. Some did try to be gentle, but the majority treated me like a sack of dog food. A few weeks after my hospital life began, the orthopedic doctors decided that my leg, which had been almost severed, was ready for casting. A fiberglass cast from the hip to the toes was molded to my leg. It felt incredibly heavy once I could feel it, although it weighed only two pounds. I later found that plaster casts weigh much more and must be kept dry. Although I could get mine wet, it still itched.

The next problem was that my foot swelled, making the cast cut into it and adding to my hurts. The orthopedic team decided to pare it down. The residents stormed into my room, terrifying me with a giant electric saw. I had never before broken any bones and had no experience with casts. I could not see what they were doing. They were joking around and said, "Don't worry, Gari, we won't cut off too much of your foot. You won't feel a thing!" I tensed my body to fight off more pain. The saw filled the room with an unbearable buzz. I remembered similar noises from the accident. I felt my cast and leg and whole body vibrate with the pressure of the blade. I braced myself for the intense pain when they slipped and cut me. Did they realize how I felt, immobile in my bed as their prisoner? I remembered all those old movies of patients loudly groaning, as their legs were amputated. The residents sawed off tiny parts of my cast around my toes, asking me each time if I felt better. I wrote on my pad that I could not tell, because of hurting in many spots. They stopped when they saw I could wiggle my toes. I was unbearably tense and wished I could cry with relief that my ordeal was over. Another challenge met and survived.

Once I was alert, I agonized about my wandering short-term memory. I felt anxious, afraid, and disoriented much of the time. If I panicked that I would forget things, my fragile memory disappeared even faster. Interestingly, after a head injury, as after a stroke, no one knows which parts of the brain will be affected. I had excellent memory of events in the past, as well as the foreign languages I spoke—French, Spanish and Italian—but very little memory of the accident. I would forget what had happened that day, or a remark someone just said to me. Neurology tested me but could give me no hope or definite answers for the future. This frustrated me incredibly; I wanted to know what my chances were and what I could be doing to help get my memories back. I hated feeling slow and stupid. I was *not* going to be a vegetable in this new life!

My mother and one of the nurses spoke French and helped me practice. Another spoke Spanish, and so I had opportunities to practice remembering simple vocabulary and grammar use in two languages. It was amazing how much more easily those languages came back to me than English, my first language. I thought, if I could remember French and Spanish, perhaps I could return to teaching after my face was remade. It would be a long time before I could walk into my shop and not shock anyone.

All this time, letters, cards and flowers were arriving

at the hospital. In the beginning, I was aware only of pain and non-pain. When I could finally see hazy snatches of the lovely arrangements of flowers, I longed to be able to smell them. After I could communicate with my Magic Slate, I asked the nurses to take some of the flowers to others on the hall who did not have any. I kept just one or two vases to enjoy from then on. It amazed me that people cared enough to send flowers to cheer my voyage of recovery.

Flowers always bring back two special memories to me. When I was a little girl, my father started a thoughtful tradition of giving me a bouquet, all of my own, to take to church each Easter. The first ones were tiny nosegays; as I grew, so did my bouquets. There would always be my favorite baby pink or yellow rosebuds, which captured my heart with their magic smell. With my nose buried in the soft velvety roses, I wished that my very own bouquet would last forever, hugged inside my heart. The sweet aroma made me feel extra specially loved.

My other strong vision and scent of flowers is from my debutante year. The Bachelors Cotillion was held on the first Thursday in December, in Baltimore's Lyric Theatre. That evening, the orchestra seats were covered by a dance floor, with red carpeted steps leading to the stage. Each debutante had an assigned theatre box, whose front was covered with wire mesh. Friends send bouquets of flowers to each debutante's house before the ball; my bouquets in boxes piled beside the staircase reached from the first floor to the second. I had never seen that many in my life, except in a florist shop, and could not believe that they were all just for me. They were delivered to the ballroom before the Cotillion and banked into the frame in front of my box, which had my name on a large card. I remember my father's pleasure and pride, escorting me to the "Monday German," as it was locally called.

As we entered, the scent of the theatre filled my whole being with the same ecstasy as my childhood bouquets. Tears pricked my eyelids and my throat closed up. I looked down and swallowed to regain my composure. My father looked at me and asked, "What is wrong? This is supposed to be a happy time."

I smiled. "I was remembering how loved I felt, when I first opened the box of my Easter bouquet. I was overwhelmed by the rosy scent. I feel the same way right now." He beamed back at me, as he began presenting his only daughter to Proper Society. After the ball, I took the train that night to return to college, loaded with bouquets in boxes for all the girls on my dorm hall. My family delivered the rest to hospitals the next day to cheer up patients without flowers. In my second life, I was glad to be able to continue the tradition of spreading pleasure with flowers.

The cards and notes were incredibly kind and encouraging, once I was able to understand them. My mother would read me each day's mail. I felt emotional and wondered why these people were saying wonderful things about me—I was just another person like anyone else. I remembered writing similar notes to others in the hospital. I never thought I would receive them myself. Death seems far away when you are healthy. Most people took time to write exceptionally thoughtful notes. I was touched by their caring, positive encouragement, their attempts to keep my hope alive.

The pain became less intense three weeks after the accident, when the tooth was removed, but I was comfortable for only about two hours out of four, between each pain shot. The nurses seemed to drag their feet, giving me injections late, which infuriated my mother. We later found out that the current medical philosophy dictated delaying drugs to avoid making the patient dependent. Unfortunately, all that policy accomplishes is to make the patient crave pain relief. Pain is hard to define for anyone else and incredibly personal. Mine went from an overall overwhelming engulfment like a tsunami to a sense of specific areas ebbing and flowing against the tide of hurt.

After the tracheostomy tube had been removed and I felt more alert, I was wheeled down to the physical therapy department to learn how to cope in the real world. Thus began one of the most difficult lessons in my new life. I was determined to be perfect but had no idea how long and how hard the journey would be. Jim Brady, who was shot with President Reagan, says they should be called "physical terrorists," and I agree. They don't try to be, but they really do hurt and push harder than you would yourself, which is sadly necessary.

For this first visit, I was shown how to strengthen my legs. I was put on a tall, hard table, sitting with my free leg hanging down. A one-pound weight was strapped onto my ankle; I was supposed to lift that weight up and down with my leg ten times. After my first attempt, I was exhausted and discouraged. I was also taught to lift hand weights to increase muscle tone. I still had not been allowed to see myself in a mirror, which might have helped me watch my progress. I had never liked exercise or sports as a child. This seemed like more torture. I had suffered through years of tennis lessons, riding lessons, dancing lessons, ballet lessons, skiing lessons and skating lessons, as well as the required playing of hockey, lacrosse, soccer, softball, and basketball in school. I thought that when I was grown I could successfully avoid all the horrors of team sports. At the age of thirty, I discovered my own sport—yoga—where I competed only against myself and felt successful. Once I was limber with yoga, other sports began to appeal to me. Physical therapy was difficult because I had been away from yoga. Although it was my least favorite part of my new life, I would learn many invaluable new skills along the way in physical therapy. It was another tool to help me become the person I was meant to be, fitting in with my new environment.

One day on rounds, after about six weeks, Dr.

Edgerton asked, "Would you like to go home, Gari?"

"Wow, I thought you would never ask!"

"We feel that you have healed enough to manage at home, providing you have someone to care for you there."

"My mother has it all arranged, just waiting for your go-ahead. I'm thrilled at long last that it will happen."

"We will need to see you back in the clinic in a few weeks. Do you know how to care for your incisions? They are healing well on your face and legs—even your 'second smile' scar around your chin looks better."

"Thank you, Dr. Edgerton. I know the steps for suture line care well by now."

"Your job at home will be to heal quickly, to be ready for the next surgery in a few months. Also, when the scars are ready, I would like you to massage them gently but firmly three times each day for five minutes, so that the scar tissue will be soft for me to work on."

"I'll look forward to the day when you can work to improve my face. Thanks!" I burst with happiness until I could tell Mum, who rapidly went into action to prepare the way for me.

The night before I left the hospital, my college roommate, Lee, came to visit, as she had almost every day. She asked, "Is there anything I can do for you?"

I jumped at the chance and asked, "Would you please wash my hair? I would love to have clean hair to go home." Lee is marvelous at taking charge and in no time she had commandeered a stretcher, pitchers, shampoo and the nurses' kitchen sink. We giggled as I shuffled and rolled across from the bed to the stretcher. She joked about how heavy I was, as she wheeled me into the hospital kitchen. We never would have thought, years ago rooming together in college, that she would be washing my hair for me under these circumstances. She asked if I would cry if she got soap in my eyes like our children? We both laughed, remembering the stage of shampoo hats and tearful "hairpoos." I inched to the edge of the stretcher as she poured water over my head. She managed to shampoo me clean, without getting any soap in my eyes. What a gift to feel clean hair again! I had no idea how Mum would manage at home without a stretcher to move me around. So many changes and adjustments would happen at home the next day. At this point, having clean hair mattered more than almost anything in the world to me. I was grateful for Lee's thoughtfulness. My priorities had changed rapidly in this new life!

Chapter 5

When the next day arrived and I was able to go home after six weeks in the hospital, I was thrilled at the chance to see familiar territory. A nurse came in to help me out of my blue and white floral cotton hospital gown and into my First Real People Clothes. The day before, Mum had brought me a soft, loose blue dress which buttoned up the front, a slip, underpants, one sock, and a shoe. I was still too thin to fill out a bra, so she had not bothered with one. The nurse and I laughed as she stood me up to adjust my clothes. My underpants slid down my hips and caught on the cast. We discussed taping them up, but she found a safety pin so I would not "drop my drawers" in public, even though I would be lying on a stretcher for the trip. I realized that I was not going to be able to wear my old clothes for a while, until I gained some weight back. My mother and stepfather had moved from the hotel near the hospital into my house, in order to supervise my care. Mum had arranged for a hospital bed to be set up in my dining room for me so I could be on the first floor. My mother, in her efficient way, had coped wonderfully with all the logistics necessary for me to return.

My mother and stepfather drove to the hospital so that she could ride back with me in the funeral home's hearse/ambulance. Because we lived in a small town, this was the only possibility to get me home, since I could not yet manage sitting in a car. What a triumph to ride in that hearse alive after such an accident! The funeral attendants, whom I knew well, as one does everyone in a small town, surprised me by their gentleness loading me on the stretcher. I wondered if they treated dead bodies this way. All the floor nurses came to say goodbye and give me words of encouragement for my next stage of healing at home. I felt almost sad at leaving them and my familiar hospital world to go into this new unknown world of home. My mother carried my current flowers, the latest cards and letters, my Magic Slate, and my collection of Brecht feeders. Otherwise, I had no possessions. I grinned with happiness as the funeral attendants wheeled the stretcher out of the hospital.

The outside real world took my breath away with its brightness. I had forgotten how sparkly the sun was outside and how richly green the early spring grass could be. I could not believe the intensity of the blue sky, when not seen through a window, and the bite of crispy true air on my skin. I felt I was discovering them all again with new eyes, like a released prisoner. The normal world of cars and shops and houses and mothers with baby carriages all looked pristinely healthy to me. Each landmark I recognized on the road home was another milepost of happiness. I was finally Going Home! By the time we drove up to my old Victorian house, I was exhausted, though relieved to see that it still looked the same. The funeral home attendants opened the doors and slid me out. I realized that it was going to be hard work for them to get me inside. My old-fashioned house had a step up to the sidewalk from the street, six steps up to my front path by the boxwood bushes, fourteen steps up to the front porch by the dogwood tree, and another step up into the house. I had counted them many times as I climbed up, with heavy groceries, teaching my children their numbers.

As I was worrying about the attendants' muscles, the front door opened and my two children came bursting out, followed by the dog and cat. My throat clutched, removing my new faint voice. I managed to smile at them as my eyes ran with tears. Everyone wanted to hug me at the same time, and my mother had to interfere to make the children take turns. Before I was lifted onto the hospital bed, which seemed miles up from the floor, I was able to pat my cairn terrier, Peggy, who wanted to be beside me but was unable to jump up that high. She immediately curled up under my bed. The Siamese cat Molly, to show her superiority over all dogs, established her own territory at the foot of the bed. One or the other guarded me from then on, day and night.

Even though I still had to live in a hospital bed, my mother made it as comforting as possible with smooth sheets (unlike the scratchy, stiff hospital ones), real blankets of soft wool, my very own baby pillow, and a favorite old plaid mohair lap rug. A bell was beside the bed to ring if I needed help. My eyes filled with tears at her tiny but overwhelmingly thoughtfully loving touches in my new reduced world. Of course, I had known all along that I would finally get home, but it was in the hazy future. I dared not think too much about it in the hospital, so as not to grow unhappy with my situation there. Now the dream had finally come true. As dreams are apt to be, of course, it was not as I imagined, but a combination of hard work, frustration and joy in each tiny achievement in my new life. Mum helped me undress. We laughed together at the safety pin. She carefully slid an old soft flannel nightgown over my head, trying not to touch any wounds. I felt surrounded by familiar secure memories, as I slipped between the smooth clean sheets. The cat began purring on the foot of my bed. I could not resist falling asleep sharing her contentment.

When I awoke at dinner time, Mum brought in a few jars of baby food—chicken, carrots, green beans, beef, squash, and applesauce. I could really choose what I wanted—only in liquid, of course—but a choice of my own for the first time. I felt silly, excited, and overwhelmed. Like a child, I did not know what to pick. She suggested chicken, carrots, and applesauce for my first meal at home—almost an "all white meal," but delicious because I could choose it by myself. I felt that there was hope for me to live again with enjoyment and pride. I had a food processor to grind up any sort of food into liquid for my Brecht feeder. My parents and Tom came in to keep me company as I squirted in my first meal. I was exhausted afterwards and easily went back to contented sleep with the cat and dog.

I settled quickly into being home. Happily, I was not awakened during the night to have my temperature taken. I reveled in the luxury of uninterrupted sleep. The sounds were much more muted and peaceful at home than in my hospital room. The dining room was a good choice for my sickroom. Everyone else made do eating at the kitchen table and I, of course, was "eating" where I was. My mother moved the dining room table against a bank of windows and put all the chairs in the attic except for two for visitors. She put the hospital bed against the wall to the living room. Instead of looking at a spartan hospital room, I now had a view of the fireplace, with a painting I loved over the mantle, hall doors to the right, and a bank of windows to the left, where I could watch the sky. The kitchen was behind the fireplace wall. I could hear almost anything or anyone in the house from my new location. In subtle ways, others' lives become more interesting when the perimeters of one's own life diminish. One becomes an unconscious "eavesdripper" (a word coined by my stepfather). My mother had given me the perfect prescription for recovery and restoration of my selfhood—a bright, sunny, cheerful room in the middle of all the household activity.

Mum hired nurses for two shifts during the day, taking night duty herself. There was much for her to schedule, arranging my life and Tom's. Emily was still living at her father's but visited regularly, though she avoided looking at my face. Luckily, friends helped out with the interminable car pools. I was afraid I would never be able to pay back all the rides if I lived to be 100! The house was inundated with food and flowers from all the thoughtful people in the small town who wanted to help. I would be writing thank you notes for years!

The new nurses were wonderfully gentle, compared to the hospital aides, as they touched and moved me—another benefit I had not expected in my challenging new world. The pain grew less and less each day, as I healed without being hustled around. The nurses were very inventive in thinking of little ways to make my life smoother and more comfortable. They lightly rolled the Q-tip with hydrogen peroxide across my facial suture lines, instead of scrubbing furiously. They showed me how the peroxide bubbled away any dirt by itself. They blotted my face with gauze instead of wiping, which had hurt and pulled the scars. Finally, a thin film of Bacitracin was rolled over the area with a Q-tip to protect the raw skin. Each day, I had dreaded suture line care in the hospital, but at home it finally felt good to be clean again!

My new routine began right away. Mum would get up and deliver my bedpan to me. Next she woke up Tom and fixed his breakfast. Then my stepfather would drive him to school, after reminding him each day to take his books and lunch. The morning nurse would arrive at 8:00 A.M. and make my breakfast, which consisted of oatmeal with liquid vitamins and bran, juice, and Red Zinger tea. Next, the nurse would wash me and clean up all my scars. By then, my mother would be ready to make her daily trip to the market, after planning the day's meals. I would nap a bit or talk to visitors until lunch. For lunch, I was lifted out of bed and put in a dining room chair by the table, to squirt some sort of liquid down my throat. My favorites were baby chicken, turkey, peas, and carrots. After a while, I had all the flavors mixed in the blender together, as I could not taste. One day as a treat, the nurse ground up pizza for me. It was not the thrill I thought it might be, though I did not tell her. I tried to keep a Brecht feeder by the bed and "drink" lots during the day, so as not to lose fluids. After lunch, my parents and I napped. Then Tom came home from school. We talked about his day, then he got a snack and went out to play. Several visitors usually arrived in the afternoon. Then my parents would watch the news on TV with me, which helped give me something besides myself to think about. The news made me aware that time does not stand still and wait for you. I felt out of touch, as if I had been in another world. I would try to sit up again, while I had my liquid dinner, if I was not too tired. The very last thing Mum did before she went to bed was to bring me my bedpan.

One night, as she was taking it out to empty, she paused at the foot of the bed and said, "You know, I have always felt dreadfully guilty that I was not able to take care of you as a baby because I was ill and incapacitated myself."

I laughed and said, "What do you think you're doing for me now!" and gestured toward the bedpan. We both giggled. From that moment we were best friends, dismissing all the years of criticism, misunderstanding, and guilt. I never knew that my mother felt that way before. It made me understand why she tried to make up for lost time by wanting me to be the best-looking and best-behaving child possible. She was finally able to laugh at her old feelings of guilt and let them go. My mother is a powerful and determined woman. She laid the foundation in my first life for the inner core of strength, upon which now I was able to depend in my second life. She knew I could never possibly manage without her in my present condition. I knew that I did not have to fight her again for my independence. It would return when I was ready and able to survive on my own. It was like being her baby all over again, except this time was fun for us both. We could relax and love and learn and laugh together. This new friendship was one of the most important gifts from my accident, for which I will always be grateful.

My hair felt dirty, which bothered me. I had always washed it every few days and longed to have at least one part of me immaculate and pretty. My mother called my hairdresser to see if she could help me. I could not manage long hair lying in bed. I looked forward to seeing her to find out how she was and what was going on in her life. I knew that she would take care of my dirty hair. Karen was concerned about how she was going to be able to wash my hair and keep me comfortable. She brought buckets, washtubs, and every possible bit of equipment she might need with her. She helped me move so that my head was on the edge of the bed and lined the area under me with plastic and towels. Mum held me in place over the basin on the chair beside the bed, while Karen poured water from a pitcher to wet my hair. I held a towel over my face so I did not get any of the healing areas wet. Then they slid me back on the bed while my hair was shampooed and pulled me over the edge again for rinsing. I felt wonderfully renewed and relaxed. I sat up to have my hair dried, but the drier's heat stung my face like fire, so Karen used a towel. Then she began looking at the parts of my scalp which had confused her as she washed it. There were many tiny circular bald spots all over my head. I later found out this was from neurological testing. One patch of hair at the side of my forehead was white. She explained that a shock to the body or a severe illness can cause hair to lose its color. I wondered how I would look in the future. I was not ready for grey hair and being crippled all at once. Karen recommended that I have my hair cut shorter to be easier to manage and keep clean with the future surgeries. I loved my long hair and hated the idea of losing another pretty part of me. She reminded me that it would grow back and that every time any hair touched my scars for a long time, it would hurt me. Sadly, I had to agree that she was right; my mother, who never liked long hair, was thrilled. I had lost most of my former self already.

I felt as if I were losing another part and wanted to sob with the finality of each scissor snip and rip. When Karen was finished cutting, I wanted to see how I looked. Mum made excuses, as she was still keeping mirrors from me, afraid that I would be depressed by my appearance. I gave up asking.

The very next day, as soon as Mum had gone to the market on her morning trip, I rang the bell by my side to call the nurse. (No one could hear my new husky voice at any distance.) When Lorraine, the morning nurse, came in, I said, "I would like to see a mirror while my mother is gone, but please do not tell her." Lorraine was caught between two determined ladies but agreed to get me a mirror. She sat on the floor beside me as I looked at my new face and watched my expression, worried that I would be upset. I steeled myself, but the face did not look nearly as dreadful as I had thought. It reminded me that truth is much kinder than imagination at times. The eyes were red and puffy and I had minimal nose and lip shapes. Despite a swollen purple road map of scars, however, it was still sort of a face. I thought, "This is not me—I do not look like raw hamburger; I am pretty." By clinging to the memory of my first face and ignoring my new limitations, I was able to avoid being upset by what the mirror showed me. Lorraine looked relieved as I smiled at her. Why was I always comforting others for my problems? I thanked her for helping and asked that she put the mirror back before my mother returned. I still felt that, with Dr. Edgerton, I would have my pretty face back soon again and be running and dancing and skiing as in my first life.

One afternoon, after I had been home about a week, the trooper investigating the accident came to interview me. He had already talked to everyone else involved. He said, "I was confused as to why your steering wheel was turned sharply to the left. Your son explained that due to the guard rail on your side, you tried at the last minute to avoid the other car by going into their lane. Whenever there is rain or snow, we have more accidents due to people who drive too fast for the conditions. We always dread bad weather." I told him what I remembered—the snow increasing, driving slowly, and suddenly seeing the huge car speeding straight at us in our lane and knowing that I could not escape. Later, my mother attended the court hearing, as I was unable to go out. The young driver was there with her parents. Despite all the havoc she caused, she was charged with driving too fast for the conditions. Surprising my family and friends, I never felt any anger or self pity, as I told what happened. In my first life, I would have been filled with rage at the unfairness. I would have tried to strike back to inflict greater pain on any person who had hurt me. Now, I felt removed and unconcerned with revenge. It was more important to me to turn this destructive event into a positive outcome for me. I felt sorry for the driver and wondered if she would spend the rest of her life with guilty memories. Once the legal aspects were settled, I wrote her to say that I did not want her to feel that I hated her for what had happened and wished that the rest of her life went smoothly.

Mum was worried about some minor fix-up jobs which needed to be done on the house. I had been living with the problems, as one does with an older house. Mum felt that if she were free from the aggravation of things not working properly, she could better use all her energy helping me heal. I had her call a friend who was a magician at fixing anything. John came right over and took care of all the problem faucets and doors. After he finished, he came in my room to visit. He was one of the few people who was not visibly shocked by my appearance, giving me hope. John said, "I talked to the guy who put out the fire in your engine after your accident. He said that he felt you were aware of him, despite not having a face. You were lucky that he came along when he did before the fire really got going." I was pleased to finally find out who had rescued me in order to thank him. John said he would come by and visit again. He had hesitated to do so before, not knowing how I was. He told my satisfied mother to call him immediately if there were anything else she needed fixed. Kind friends were a constant joyful surprise when I was incapable of giving.

After a few weeks, I was driven back to the hospital with Mum in the funeral home's hearse/ambulance to have my cast cut off—a Red Letter Day for me! As I was wheeled on my stretcher into the orthopedic cast room by the funeral attendant, I felt twinges of fear remembering my "sawing off the toe area experience." Instead of three residents to do the job, I had a huge orderly with a welcoming smile.

I said right away, "I'm terrified of being cut."

He shook his head. "I am the expert—those residents have no idea what they are doing with casts." He had put on my cast weeks before when I was not alert enough to remember him. He took out his electric saw and in just a second, with buzzing and light pressure, the cast was cut down both sides. He raised the top; the air felt freezing on my naked leg. Next, he gently raised my leg to pull out the back of the cast. He put the two halves together so that I could hold them and feel how light the cast really was. It weighed only two pounds, but it had seemed like a giant lead weight on my leg! I raised my head to look down at my china-white shriveled leg. A huge ugly purple scar snaked across my knee where the engine had severed it. I was terrified to move my poor leg in case it might crumple apart without the support of the cast. The other leg looked fat and strong in comparison. When the orthopedic doctor entered, Mum asked why my feet would still be hurting me. He checked my legs and took more x-rays, discovering that both feet had also been broken. They were not noticed in the rush to correct the more obvious problems in the Emergency Room. I had felt that my feet had no right to hurt; now I knew they did, though they had healed by themselves while I was immobile.

Next I was wheeled to Physical Therapy by the funeral attendant. There I was fitted for a brace with Velcro straps, to remove at night. It was of canvas, with stiff metal stakes fitted into it around the sides, but it seemed flimsy to me. I was terrified to use my fragile leg without the protection of the cast. The Physical Therapist reassured me that I would not break again. Then I was measured and fitted for my first crutches and made to stand up on them. I felt weak standing alone. I was convinced that my legs would break underneath me, but, amazingly, they did not. I had been dreaming of my First Step for ages, but it was nasty pain, not fun. Each movement was exhausting, hurtful work, making me long to return to the easy stretcher or wheelchair. I felt like the stiff Tin Man in the *Wizard of Oz*. Mum praised me for walking, reminding me that I did not have to do it all in one day. I was told to practice every day on the crutches to strengthen my arms. The funeral attendant then wheeled me out into his hearse/ambulance and drove us home. I was thankful that I was going back to my own house away from the hospital again.

Slowly, I built up stamina on those wretched crutches, forcing my stiff legs to move. Mum and the nurse would lift me out of bed and position me with my crutches. One would guard each side of me as I pushed each leg forward and moved a crutch. At first, I could only manage the five steps from my bed to the chair before collapsing. Walking hurt my feet, legs, hips, arms, neck, and shoulders in stabs at the time and aches afterwards. I had to watch my legs and will each one to move for me. If I forgot to look, I lost my concentration and did not move. Mum suggested that I try for one more step each day. It helped again to have little, reachable kindergarten goals. My greatest triumph was managing to walk on them the twenty-odd steps from my hospital bed to the bathroom without calling anyone for help. I was even able to turn to position myself over the toilet and sit down all by myself. I never thought that it would be such a thrill to use a toilet! I hated the indignity of bedpans and the difficulty of using them in a prone position. Having someone else wipe my bottom made me feel dirty and out of control. I felt the same sense of accomplishment that a child feels when toilet training has succeeded—all grown up and invincible! This feeling vanished quickly, however, when I tried to get up and could not. My arms were too weak to pull myself to standing. I had to call Mum for help. We laughed that I was only half a grownup.

I missed my solace of books intensely. My mother had been proud when I learned to write my name at the age of four, so that I could have my very own library card. She read to me from the time I was tiny, and I could not wait until I was grownup enough to read by myself. I knew my alphabet before going to school but can still remember the magic moment in first grade at Bryn Mawr School when our teacher, Miss Clark, told the class that the combinations of letters we saw meant real words which we knew. The huge light bulb went on in my head at that moment—I had never put it all together until she explained that Dick, Jane, Sally, and Spot were in a story we could read all by ourselves. From then on, I had not only the pleasure of Mum reading to me, but also the delight of discussing what I had read alone with others.

Whenever I tried to read now, it hurt my eyes after two or three words. Mum took me to my ophthalmologist, who said it could take up to a year for my vision to return to normal after such an accident. I was depressed to hear of another long unknown wait to endure. I still found it hard to concentrate with my short attention span. Television bored me. The newspaper was hard for me to hold up to see without arm strength. I had always looked forward to reading the funny papers and was anxious to catch up on my favorite strips, but I was disappointed to find that nothing had changed. The characters were in the same situations as they had been months before, unlike real life. I decided to spend my precious reading time on more worthwhile books.

I was totally alone with my thoughts for the first time, without my wall of books to shield me from real life. My new situation had removed all impediments to my quest for the core and meaning of my changed life. I realized that the values in my first life—money, social status, and appearance—were worthless to me now. My new priorities were more old-fashioned—peace and unity with my surroundings, integrity, love, harmony of mind, and good health. I thought of the quote by the Stoic philosopher Seneca: "The good things which belong to prosperity are to be wished, but the good things that belong to adversity are to be admired." I wanted to read inspiring books to help me savor the tiny satisfying pleasures enriching my new life, such as the beauty of a flower, the pleasure of harmonious music, the comfort of my cat snuggling next to me, the pride my mother radiated with each of my new accomplishments, and the joy my son showed as he realized how helpful he now was to me. I found it almost impossible to meditate, which I had been doing for several years. Whenever I tried, I lost concentration. My life felt empty, just sleeping and healing. I had no choice but to learn to know my real self. I realized I had to make the best of it. The more determination and discipline I used to conquer my challenges, the sooner it would be over and I could do all the things I had done before. I asked Mum as she sorted my stacked up mail to look for my copy of *The Daily Word* by Unity. Perhaps I could begin reading the positive thoughts for the day and start meditating again. Though it was hard to focus my eyes, I wanted to know what was written and persisted to read the three or four paragraphs of inspiration and then meditate or pray on a part of what was said each day. Next, Mum found my notebook of quotations I had loved and copied down over the years. I read one inspiring quote a day and tried to memorize it, such as this thought by Dorothy MacLean: "Being thankful produces peace and worrying produces more worry and unrest. Try to find some good in everything today and peace will stay with you." For each meditation I tried repeating just one affirmation, such as "I am able to walk easily and well," as long as I could keep it in focus in my mind. Slowly I built up to the point where I could read a short magazine article or a page of a book and meditate for a few minutes. I felt proud with each new inch into my second life.

For some time one of the most helpful parts of my life had been my journal, which I had kept for years, writing down all my feelings and hiding them from the world. When I began, I used an old spiral notebook left over from school supplies and mainly made lists of what I did that day. I became discouraged and felt what I was doing was stupid. At a seminar, I asked Dorothy MacLean, one of the founders of Findhorn, how she had written such inspiration for others in her journal. She told me that the important thing was to write each day, not to judge what I wrote and enjoy what enfolded over the years. I returned bolstered by such valuable advice and determined to teach myself to write of my true feelings, which I had ignored as socially unacceptable. Slowly my writing evolved into a melange of my secret emotions. I made my journal into a special kindness for myself, searching for a new prettily covered blank book weeks before I finished the last page in my current one. The journal I was using before my accident had a lovely blue paisley cover and lined pages, which helped me in my erratic writing in the hospital bed. Since I played the cheerful patient role to the public, I savored being able to write away the frustration and anguish carved into my hidden heart. Every week, I made myself go back and reread what had bothered me that past week. Many of the problems which seemed insurmountable when encountered dissolved during a week's time, giving me greater courage to continue rebuilding my shattered life.

Gradually, I discovered my inner self, which had been buried under years of layers of "shoulds" and "doing the done things." I became aware that I would not compromise my values ever again to fit into a crowd. I believed in the purity of loving others as I loved myself. I resolved to shower kindnesses on others, as well as myself, in the future. In my first life, I had put my needs last and had resented others for my self-effacement. I savored the prayer of Saint Francis of Assisi, which I remembered singing in church:

Lord, make me an instrument of thy Peace.
Where there is hatred, let me sow love;
Where there is injury, pardon;
Where there is doubt, faith;
Where there is despair, hope;
Where there is sadness, joy;
Where there is darkness, light.

O Divine Master, grant that I may
* not so much seek*
to be consoled as to console;
Not so much to be understood,
* as to understand;*
Not so much to be loved, as to love.
For it is in giving that we receive,
It is in pardoning that we are pardoned,
It is in dying that we are born again
* to eternal life.*

Chapter 6

Another incredible gift from the accident was the reversal of an enzyme deficiency. The problem had begun four years earlier when I had the flu several times in close succession and was heavily dosed with antibiotics. The drugs decimated the ability of pancreatic enzymes to digest all sugar, corn, and milk products. I suffered from dysentery for a year, with doctors trying many tranquilizers and telling me that my mind was the cause. My mother convinced me to try one last doctor at the University of Pennsylvania, who persisted in testing until she found the solution — disaccharidase deficiency — usually present from birth. After that, I learned how to eat and cook without any milk, corn, or sugar products in my diet. I spent hours reading every label in the supermarket, and I found that most foods we ate contained one or more of my forbidden categories. I had to be basic. I missed tea and coffee dreadfully, but I hated the taste without cream and sugar. I longed to drink a case of Coca-Cola all by myself. I dragged without energy for several weeks as my body adjusted to its new diet. I despaired that I could never eat normally again.

My yoga teacher, Yusuf, taught me about nutrition and new substitutions, such as Red Zinger herb tea, which I soon adored. At first I cooked regular meals for the family and separate meals for myself. I tired of that rapidly and began combining foods. My family drank milk on their own, but there was none in my cooking. I had to make every recipe from scratch. I baked bread with water and honey, instead of sugar or milk. Casseroles hid unusual ingredients and desserts included only honey as a sweetener. I craved cheese and butter—but even a tiny taste would punish me with overwhelming cramps and dysentery. The family became more healthy sharing my diet, but my daughter never forgot the last box of Hostess Ho Ho's I bought. Both children hated our new diet and traded their healthy lunches for sugar snacks at school whenever possible. Needless to say, they were ecstatic when they learned after the accident that I could eat normally—once I graduated from liquids. The shock to my body made the pancreas produce the necessary enzymes to digest all foods again. This freedom made my diet more nutritious, as milk could be added to liquify foods without my becoming sick. I decided to eat milk and corn products again, but not sugar. I liked feeling good all the time without dependence upon sugar highs. I could not wait to enjoy real-people food with real teeth. After leaving the hospital, I had weekly checkups with my general practitioner, who weighed me and supervised my diet to gain weight. I felt as if I were a child trying to achieve an impossible goal. I kept squirting food into my throat, but it seemed to take forever to gain even one ounce. It was a Major Red Letter Day, after months of stuffing myself, when I finally reached one hundred pounds on the scale!

Amazingly, all sorts of people, from whom I had not heard in years, surfaced and wrote or called to encourage me. It was such a surprise and pleasure to realize that my life's network was concerned. The assortment ran from distant relations, old school friends, and people I had worked with, to friends from places where I had lived years before. I had been brought up always to think of others first. I had never been in the position of being the one considered. Being the object of so much attention, of which I was not sure I was worthy, made me focus on my past perspectives. I had not felt worthwhile in my first life; I had tried to do the proper things as I had been taught, but not always with my heart in the action. My ego and self-concern lurked behind and motivated my good deeds. My perspective of life was different now. Although I constantly had to be aware of myself and my limitations, I had gained a shimmer of empathy with others. Before, I had removed my inner self from people. Now, I was looked on as the essence of compassion, due to my own real suffering or what the viewer imagined I was suffering. I was not sure that this second pair of shoes fit me.

One very dear friend came to visit soon after I was home. I remember his coming in the room, averting his eyes and going to the chair to my left, carefully looking down as he sat. He had been a good friend through thick and thin, and I had missed seeing him. He had written me lots of letters in the interim. He reluctantly raised his hazel eyes, as a look of relief brightened his face. He said, "I have been afraid to see you because of the contrast. I wanted to remember you as you were but could not put off visiting any more. You really do not look as mutilated as I had imagined. I'm glad I waited until you were somewhat healed."

I laughed. "I'm still me inside this new outer shell. I'm glad that you feel that we can still be friends because I missed your wit and insight. Some friends are lost, due to my appearance. The loss makes me sad, but people have to accept me the way I am now. I have to wait for the doctors to change anything else. The most frustrating facet for me is my lack of independence."

He said, "You have always been a giver and now you have to learn the hardest lesson of all — to receive without being able to give anything back. You are already giving by the sparkles of courage radiating from your eyes as we talk." That was an invaluable lesson for me. I remembered his words whenever I would find myself falling back into the same old pattern of feeling guilty for not giving back, or resenting having to depend on someone else.

Mary, my shop manager, had been to see me every

few days. One day she arrived with a purpose and a present all wrapped for me. I excitedly opened a book of inspirational quotations, with a special one for each day of the year. In the front, she and Louise had written, "Keep looking on the bright side, Gari!"

"What a thoughtful present just when I need it; thank you so much." The book turned out to be a new window for my daily meditations. I still think of Mary and Louise every day when I read it.

Mary said, "We have to work together again, as there are decisions I can not make alone. You need to start to enter the real world."

"I don't feel ready to handle the shop, but I guess one never does," I said. Mary kindly began with two small decisions on how much to reorder of certain clothes and gifts. I had difficulty remembering figures and qualities that she mentioned, but she patiently repeated the facts until I understood. Ironically, in the past, I had anticipated eventually supervising my shop or shops from a distance. But I never thought it would happen due to my unacceptable appearance. I felt healthier, busying my mind with sales and projections rather than only coping with pain and survival.

There were no vacations in my new life. My main job was to heal so that I would ready for the next cancellation for surgery at a moment's notice. It was amazing how my day filled up with just being washed and fed, physical therapies, and incessant practice to regain the physical and mental memories I lost.

The only physical therapist in town was at the nursing home, so I went there to learn how to walk and strengthen my legs. The musty medical smells assaulted me as I entered the first day. I remembered a friend who had to live there for several months after a stroke and how she detested it. It would be horrid not to be able to escape from those smells or the depressed, drugged people. My friend was most bothered by the fact that she was tied into her bed each night, totally losing her independence. I felt thankful to be more alert and active than the residents; visitors were privileged and apart.

Although Susan, the physical therapist, tried to make the exercises fun and painless, I found it hard to believe that this period would ever end and I could lead a normal life again. I felt terribly alone in an uncertain future. I longed for anyone who had recovered from the same sort of experience to give me hope when I felt discouraged. No Hero existed for me. Even talking to someone who really understood would help me. When I felt hopeless, I would remember my unwavering purpose of overcoming all my limitations and challenges. I would show all those negative thinkers what a positive view could do to a shattered body and life!

In the Physical Therapy Room, I sat on a table while successively heavier weights were put on my ankles. I had to raise and lower my weak legs to improve my muscle tone. Although I had little or no feeling in my legs and feet, my knees clicked with each stab of painful movement, beginning new aches. I dreaded the difficult work more and more, both at Physical Therapy and at home, practicing with weights and Theraband loops, which are wide pieces of stretchy rubber fabric used for muscle resistance, either tied into a loop for legs or held in the hands. I was afraid that my weak legs would break again. I wanted to learn to walk and get off the crutches, but it felt hopeless. I knew I could not permit myself to stop, despite my fears.

Later, when Susan began teaching me to walk, I was positioned between two long parallel bars. I thought how silly—I could just walk without holding on. I was sure I remembered. I had practiced long enough on crutches. I found, however, with the first step, that I had totally forgotten when to put down a toe or a heel. My walking was stiff, jerky, and awkward. I was frustrated and embarrassed by the loud ticking, like a time bomb, in my legs as I moved. Every click sent a new shot of pain through the knees, and I just wanted to lie down and give up. Susan reminded me to place my toes and heels up and down with each slow step; hesitantly, I followed her directions. After lots of laborious practice between the parallel bars, I graduated to try a real walk outside the bars. I stood right next to them, so that I could grab hold if I needed balance—my sense of balance had departed along with other memories. I tried a triumphant march, which lasted for two steps before I had to grab for support.

Susan said, "Gari—what about your arms?" I had held my arms tensely clutched to my sides except when lurching for the bar. I thought I had moved normally but was still afraid of breaking. She laughed. "You are supposed to swing your arms as you walk—don't you remember?" I did not, so we went into arm-swinging lessons. It was really difficult to time the swinging of arms in opposite rhythm to that of the legs walking. I was exhausted after my interminable half-hour of Physical Therapy that day. I wondered if the doctors were correct when they whispered to my mother that I would never walk again. I had pretended not to hear, but I remembered. How could I put myself through this torture? Was it really worth it?

The next morning, the nurse braced me with her body for walking practice. I tried to protest, but she smiled and said, "I will be right here with you." How could I not try a few steps for her? I concentrated on my slow-motion moves. I was pleasantly surprised that it was not as hurtful as the day before. I began another odyssey, though I still thought that I might never learn to walk again. I practiced seemingly forever without results. One day, after many weeks of laboring, I mastered it, without thinking how to make each step. I thought, if walking took all this work, how amazing that babies can do it effortlessly, after just a little practice. I marvelled at all the wonders ahead of me—dancing, riding, skating, sailing, skiing. I was rather intimidated to think of trying any of them, after the length of time it took me to walk. Susan assured me that I had been through the worst; the other abilities would come more easily to me now that I had passed the first hurdle.

Once I could take an unplanned step, Tom and I made a game out of walking. He would keep right by my side with his arm around my waist, so that I could lean on him if I lost my balance. He was just the right size for me to put my elbow on his shoulder. We would start at the front door and walk the length of the house, as he called out "Left, Right!" like a drill sergeant. At first I only hopped and hobbled halfway before I was exhausted and gave up. Every time I wanted to stop or became discouraged, Tom would remind me, "You are a Big Girl now; you can do it!" I remembered saying the same sort of thing to him as a baby. How our roles were reversed in my new life and what a gentle teacher my son was!

Once I could walk and stand unaided, my greatest desire was fulfilled. Mum decided that I could manage a shower instead of sponge baths. I was terrified of falling and breaking on wet tiles, but I longed to really feel squeaky-shower-clean again. Mum and Tom stood on either side with their arms around me for balance, as we slowly climbed up the stairs. I had to keep stopping to rest after every three or four steps—what a change from running up and down them before! My shower stall was large enough for two people and had a seat, so Mum, after undressing me, offered to get in with me. But I was determined to try it alone. I grabbed at the soap dish for balance as the warm cleansing water hit my body. What would I do if I fall and break again! It was worth the fear to be clean again. I envisioned the water washing away all the pain and injury, so that I could walk out of the shower perfectly healed. I felt weak and shaky but ecstatic despite the shortest shower on record. I had triumphantly passed another milestone. It was worth every second! I could hope and believe in myself again! Mum dried me off gently and helped me dress again. I was exhausted and had to sit on the steps and slide down one at a time to return to the first floor and my welcome bed. I reveled in the knowledge that I had passed another barrier on my own!

Slowly but surely my mouth healed. One day Mum decided I was ready for a cup and spoon. When she brought them to me with my oatmeal and tea, I was startled. "I've wanted to try real eating forever, but I'm afraid I'll hurt my mouth by using them," I told her.

"I looked through all your spoons to find you one with very round edges. The cup is smooth also. You have to start getting used to eating normally sometime. I'll help you begin. Do you remember what to do?" She guided the cup into my hands and waited.

I lifted the tea to where I remembered my mouth had been to sip it. "Oh no," I cried as I poured tea down my chin, "I can't feel anymore. I don't know when the cup is close enough for drinking."

Mum mopped me up. "You'll get better with practice. It's much easier for me this time helping you learn, without your fierce independence, which always interfered. I think you must be relaxed because you know you did it before. In the past, you were determined to show the world you could succeed without my help." She handed me a tiny spoonful of oatmeal. I tried valiantly to get it in my mouth, but hit my cheek and burst into tears. I had dreamed of this day for so long. I was a dismal failure. "Oatmeal is not worth crying over," said Mum as she hugged me. "I'll get you a mirror, so you can watch as you practice." With the mirror it was a little easier, but not an instant step back into the former life I remembered. I had to work with every spoonful for months before I could manage not to spill. Even though I felt the Brecht feeders were difficult, using two hands on a syringe was easier for me than aiming one with a spoon. But the world was suddenly within my reach again. I *knew* I could do it!

Chapter 7

I was excited the day we received the great news of a cancellation in Dr. Edgerton's schedule. The new specialist had arrived, so they could begin restructuring my jaw and making gums inside my mouth. I was happy that things were finally going to happen, but I was terrified at the prospect of hurting intensely again. I wondered if I would have enough endurance to go through it all. I knew I had no choice, however. My face could not function without a nose or a mouth.

Mum drove me to the University of Virginia for my evaluation before the next surgery. We waited together in the Craniofacial Clinic, which was different from the usual sterile medical waiting rooms. This thoughtfully planned room had a forest-green thick carpet, soft beige fabric-covered couches and chairs, pretty green floral curtains, and healthy green plants in a divider across the middle of the room. The lighting was soft and recessed, not accentuating any patient's deformity. On the walls were cheerfully bright nature paintings by a local artist whom I knew. There was an abundance of current magazines, a big toy chest, and a large clean restroom with a counter for diaper changing. The room exuded life and healing. I felt as comfortable and as welcome as if I were visiting a friend.

In the examination room, Dr. Edgerton introduced me to Dr. Robert Chuong, who had a similar gentle touch. They examined my face meticulously. Their plans for this surgery were to refracture my jaws to make them fit together, reconstruct my cheeks, smooth lumps from the broken bones around my eyes, and start shaping lips. This would all be internal work. My outside would not change yet. I found it incredibly frustrating to have to wait for the foundation to be built; all I wanted was the final outer appearance. I would be in the hospital for seven to ten days this time. In the future, a nose would be made for me and teeth would be fitted into my new jaws, then lips would be grafted and shaped in several steps. Each time, the scars would be reduced as much as possible. To have the best final results, a period of at least six months needed to lapse between surgeries to allow for proper recovery and healing of tissues. I could not help feeling hopeful for the future after listening to their careful plans. Next, photographs were taken in black and white, then color, of my face at all angles. I appreciated the compassion of the photographer demonstrated by not reacting to my ugly appearance. What a totally opposite experience from photography sessions during my modeling days!

I felt lucky to be a patient of Dr. Edgerton's. He had an outstanding medical background; he had been at Valley Forge General Hospital, where he worked with early pioneers in plastic surgery on soldiers after World War II, at Johns Hopkins Hospital, and at the University of Virginia Hospital, and he had earned numerous medical honors and awards. He had organized, started and directed the Craniofacial Surgery Programs at Johns Hopkins and the University of Virginia. These included a group of plastic surgeons, neurosurgeons, oral surgeons, orthodontists, geneticists, pediatricians, speech pathologists, psychologists, ophthalmologists, otolaryngologists, occupational therapists, and social workers, plus a kind and compassionate coordinator to put each patient and family at ease. In their team work, the clinic was able to deal with all aspects of a patient's deformity, in kind and thoughtful ways. Patients never felt as if they were numbers—but rather important people with needs and wants to be considered. Dr. Edgerton was a pioneer in grafting techniques, head and neck reconstruction, hand reconstruction, nerve flap repair, eye repositioning, breast augmentation, the use of major craniofacial operations in infants and small children, treatment of transsexualism and other gender disorders, integrated treatment for facial paralysis, and investigation of the psychological aspects of altering body image by plastic surgery. He was a member of numerous medical societies, had served on important national committees and editorial boards, and had been a visiting professor of plastic surgery in India, Rochester, Washington, Chicago, Yale, and Toronto. I had read a book a few years earlier, *A Face For Me*, by Debbie Diane Fox, concerning Dr. Edgerton's transformation of a girl's disfigured face, involving movement of her eyes from the sides to the front of her face and construction of fingers from her toes. I never dreamed that I would be needing his expertise in the same way as Debbie, but here I was, grateful to have such a qualified surgeon.

On the big day, Mum drove me back to the University of Virginia Hospital. The nurses on the plastic surgery floor were as kind as ever, saying how much better I looked and how smoothly I was walking, making me feel proud of all my hard work. Because of the many repeat surgeries in this specialty, patients get to know each nurse well, unlike on the other floors where a patient appears only once. Nurses become separate caring, dedicated individuals, instead of the impersonal group one first perceives. I greeted the same overworked, kind, and compassionate residents, and I met the new medical students assigned to me. I was in a different room on the other side of the floor but, luckily, had a window bed. I had a roommate this time, too—a cute young girl, also a patient of Dr. Edgerton's. It was nice to have someone to talk to, though I brought books to read.

The night before the surgery, I read, prayed, and meditated. I was given a pill for sleep which helped, though I woke up with the sunrise. The large orange sun gave me hope that it would all be over with soon, making me better. I found it hard to make small talk with Mum, who came to sit with me before I went down to the operating room. I would have preferred to meditate but did not want to be rude. I probably could not have concentrated anyway because I was anxious about hurting again. I was given pills and a shot to relax me, as the nurse put a shower cap over my hair. The orderly came too soon—it is always too soon or too late. I was not ready—but would I ever be? I got the old familiar terrified feeling in the pit of my stomach, and I wanted to vomit my fear away. All the nurses came in to wish me luck. Mum walked with me and the orderly as far as she was allowed, then squeezed my clammy hand and kissed me, saying, "Don't worry, Darling, everything will be fine."

I thought crossly, "That sure is easy for you to say since you are not the one to be carved up," but I kept my chattering jaws clenched. The ominous green doors of the operating suite swung open. The orderly wheeled me inside as I shook with terror.

I asked the orderly for a blanket when he wheeled me into the waiting alcove outside the operating room. For some reason, all the air-conditioning vents in the world seemed to be directed at my stretcher. I hated to be cold as well as nervous. The orderly came back with a blanket, which helped a little. The shakes ominously continued. I tried to use yoga breaths and count five to inhale and five to exhale. I could manage only a count of three. I was shivery nervous. Dr. Lambruschi, one of the residents, came in to check on me; he reassured me that I would be fine, which was thoughtful but did not take away my tremors. Next, a nurse came for my arm to start my I.V. I hate needles anywhere and have always been a baby about "getting stuck." Some nurses are gentle and thoughtful, while others jab in their blunt needles like battering rams. I prayed for a gentle person and she was. I held my breath and hardly felt the stick, though I was still inundated with fear and shaking with nervousness. Next, she wheeled me into the operating room, where she and Dr. Lambruschi helped me move onto the cold, hard, and comfortless operating table, with no blanket or sheets. They said I would be warmer soon, as they started wrapping me with sterile sheets. I was still freezing with icy terror. The lights were blinding. My ears were assaulted by loud noises of the surgical team's preparation. Next Drs. Edgerton and Chuong arrived and talked cheerily to me for a few minutes about the procedure for that day—jaws, cheeks, lips, and orbits. I tried to control my shivering as I listened to them. They each reached out and patted my shoulder and said I would be all right, gestures which should have helped me feel a little more confident. Few doctors today have that wonderful caring, healing touch, which cannot be taught but can only be learned from a mentor by osmosis. I thought how lucky the doctors who had studied under Dr. Edgerton and I were to have him in our lives. Next, the anesthesia drip was started. I felt the yucky familiar aluminum taste in my throat, counted to ten, said "Here I go," and slipped away into obscurity.

When I awoke in the recovery room, the hurt was much worse than I remembered. My head was covered with bulky bandages. It felt as if a sledgehammer had been pounding on it. My abdomen burned with icy pain. When I tried to talk and ask for pain medication, my jaw would not move. I was given a few sips of water with a Brecht feeder and wheeled back to my room, where Mum was waiting. Mum got a nurse to give me some codeine and left, telling me to rest. I was glad to sleep, to avoid the tremendous encircling pain.

When I opened my eyes the next day, there were five lovely vases of flowers just for me! "What a treat," I thought, between stabs of pain. I looked in the bed table mirror to see why I hurt. I saw a shocking Frankenstein head covered with bandages—certainly that could not be me! I wondered what it would feel like to live in a healthy body again. I wanted to slip back into sleep and make it all go away.

Later, Drs. Chuong and Lambruschi came to check and to change dressings. By then my jaw had swelled to the size of a massive case of mumps. I could even see my drool constantly slip out of my mouth when I looked down. I must have had an accusing look in my eyes, as Dr. Lambruschi said seriously, "Gari, this will be the worst; I promise it will get better from now on. No one would ask you to kiss them while you look like a chipmunk. You know we wouldn't leave you unkissable." I wanted to laugh, though it hurt to move any part of my face.

Dr. Chuong told me that he had refractured my jaw twice. He was not pleased with the results the first time, hence the longer seven-hour surgery. The jaw was wired in place and covered with clear plastic splints until it healed. I had to continue with the Brecht feeders. My cheeks were reshaped, and all the broken bones smoothed out as much as possible around my eyes. They took a skin graft from my abdomen to make sulcus or gum tissue around the new jaw inside my mouth. (The abdomen is the first choice of a skin donor site, because it does not have as much hair as other parts of the body.) The area in the lower front of my mouth was packed with gauze coated with strong-smelling and -tasting Balsam of Peru—a South American herb for healing. Dr. Lambruschi told me jokingly that they took two of the seven hours of surgery deciding on the location from which to take the graft. They chose a special spot and direction so that I could wear a cut-up bikini. When I saw the area, as they changed the dressing, I said, "You Guys need a fashion consultant in the operating room! This scar would be in the wrong spot for any bikini!" The scar was a long thin ribbon starting below my navel, snaking across the abdomen to curve over my hipbone. It hurt and pulled where it ran over the unprotected bone and took forever to heal. Any clothing pressure or movement bothered me for a long time; I learned to adjust myself gingerly. Dr. Edgerton called in an otolaryngologist, who opened up my nasal passages and examined my voicebox for damage while I was under anesthesia. Now they hoped that I would be able to breathe and swallow more easily. Dr. Chuong suggested pinning a towel around my neck to catch the drooling; he did not know how long it would last. I felt and knew I looked truly revolting this time.

I was depressed. I could feel my memory diminished again, due to the anaesthesia. I later found out from neurology that this was normal and "might" return, but they did not know. I wanted definite answers, but it was hard to ever receive one. Healing is a process of wait and see, while you work hard at it and hope for the best results. I also found it frustrating to try to read because I lost my concentration. I felt as if I had taken several steps backward instead of forward. As always, I found solace in my quote book, which opened to two appropriate ones. Magically, I read, "What lies behind us and what lies before us are tiny matters compared to what lies within us" (Ralph Waldo Emerson) and "Never look down to test the ground before taking your next step! Only he who keeps his eye fixed on the far horizon will find his right road" (Dag Hammarskjold). I had been looking for a road to open in front of me back into my first life. I had to accept that my first face, family, and career were erased or changed. I had to keep an open mind in order to see the new doors in front of me or the unnoticed windows at my sides for me to enter with my new face, single-parent status, and absentee shop management. Dag Hammarskjold's quote reminded me that I was still afraid of falling— literally. I must decide upon my new horizon and road for my altered life and forge ahead with courage.

Although my recovery was difficult, at least I knew the outlines of hospital life. I could not wait to have real teeth again and bite into an apple. I was about as far from that as possible, with a swollen jaw wired, packed, and covered with plastic forms. Drool dripped from my mouth with dreadful regularity. This was the most humiliating aspect of my new appearance. The drool eroded all my self-assurance. Drooling was what people out of control did. I was proud of being in control and being admired. Now I felt ugly and alone. Could I be strong enough to endure and survive this stage? My emotions swerved up and down.

I enjoyed watching the sunrise each morning out my window. Shortly after, the nurse would arrive to take temperatures and blood pressures. I would push the buttons to raise the head of my bed up to a sitting position and wait for breakfast, which was never very exciting. I had been spoiled at home having food which I chose. Now I was stuck with liquid oatmeal, soup, or liquid Jell-o. I had brought Red Zinger tea bags with me and kept a cup by my bed to "drink." For breakfast, I would have juice and liquid oatmeal. Then the nurse would do suture care, removing the bandages on my abdomen, cleaning the scars with peroxide, and putting Bacitracin and then new bandages on them. There was not much to be done for the mouth until the packing was removed. I had to be careful to squirt the Brecht feeder way back into my throat to miss the new incisions in my mouth.

In the mornings, Mum would arrive for the day, and the doctors would come on rounds to see patients. After the beds were changed by the aides, an early lunch was served, and then I tried to nap. It hurt my head to lie flat, so I always kept the head of the bed elevated. My mouth and jaw throbbed to their own rhythm of pain, despite the codeine. Sleep was my only escape. My tongue was nicked but intact, despite my worries that it would be a casualty of this surgery. New ripples of pain began if I ran it around the smooth plastic splints enveloping my jaw. All my energy was concentrated on avoiding pain. Dinner was early, then the nurses would clean my sutures as I tried not to flinch. After the evening visitors' hour, it was "lights out." We were awakened during the night for temperature-taking and medicines. One never really gets to rest in a hospital—there is always commotion and noise in the halls or someone coming in the room to clean it just as the patient has managed to fall asleep. Sleep is intermittent at best in a hospital.

Several times during doctors' rounds, Dr. Chuong removed the packing from my gums and looked at the graft, which he assured me was progressing well. I did not agree, when I saw the yards of gauze with my skin still attached, which he pulled out with tweezers. It seemed such a waste to take all that skin from my abdomen and have it slough off inside my mouth—especially since my abdomen site was intensely painful.

Slowly the jaw swelling went down, but not the drooling. I was afraid of spending the rest of my life with a towel pinned around my neck to catch yucky drool, as the world stared at me with horror. I did not want my new life to be that of a hermit; it was devastating not to know when it would stop. The drooling was just like the pain—it would not have been as bad if I only knew the time limit. Then I could say, "I will be strong and not give up until it ends in thirty minutes." Not knowing when it will be over makes it overwhelming and discouraging. I grasped at every straw of temporary relief, however long it lasted. I wondered if I could ever run and feel the enjoyment and push of the wind in my face again. Little lost pleasures increased in value as they became memories.

Finally, I had healed enough to have some of the packing permanently taken out of my mouth. An orderly wheeled me in a chair to the Plastic Surgery Department. Each time these journeys were less painful, but they were still full of staring people, which I hated. There was no room for the wheelchair in the waiting room, so I was parked in a line of patients in the utilitarian corridor. I felt we were all like miserable caged animals at the mercy of zookeepers. I wondered which reality was valid.

Luckily, I did not have to wait long to be wheeled into an examining room to hide myself. Dr. Chuong gently examined my mouth and took a long time painlessly pulling out the packing over the grafted gums. My mouth felt cold and empty without the protection of packing. I was still drooling and asked when it would stop; he said again that he did not know, but that it should get better. I was glad I could go home to heal in peace, before seeing him in two weeks to have more packing removed. Would life ever be fun again?

Chapter 8

I longed for my former independence. It was a long, laborious process becoming my second self inside and out. I had to not only relearn physical and mental abilities in new ways for survival, but also craft and shape the person I was to be. My first personality was constantly remolded by what people wanted me to be. I used to change like a chameleon, if I felt I was not fitting in. Now, I was physically prevented from performing my old roles. I was forced to watch life go by. I thought about other people's behavior and morals. I could decide what I would and would not accept, instead of adapting to others. With my second chance at life, I determined to hold fast to my own beliefs and ideals. I kept true to loving others as I wished to be loved, and I found myself showered with wonderful people and events. I no longer worried about making others' lives perfect. Facing my own recovery consumed all of my thought and time.

One of the lessons my experiences taught me was that it is better to show others the way to help themselves, instead of doing it all *for* them. Being led through physical therapy, which no one else could do for me, caused me to never again take for granted all the abilities from my first life. Each was too hard-won this time. At one time I grieved that I would never regain my walking; then I learned to manage even stairs, although only one-legged like a child, with a bannister to hold for balance. My perseverance was paying off, slowly but surely. I began to understand how appreciated accomplishments are when they are hard-earned.

After the jaw surgery, it was lovely to walk up my steps all by myself, albeit on my crutches. The trip home exhausted me. I thought how ironic that I always felt youthfully invincible before the accident. Any weakness used to surprise me. Now they were commonplace. It was the usual hot, muggy summer in Virginia. My old house was fairly cool without air conditioning if I kept it closed up. My mother, however, worried about my healing in the heat and thought a change of environment would be good.

Additionally, Mum was ready to go home; it was hard to believe that she and my stepfather had been living away from home for almost six months taking care of me. I was anxious to start being on my own again, as well. We decided that after my stitches were out and I was more mobile, she would drive my son and me to Baltimore and then return to Philadelphia. Tom was to leave for camp in Maine, and I was to accept my stepmother's invitation to stay with her at the beach. I had not thought of a real vacation since forever. It was splendidly uplifting for me to have a non-surgical event to anticipate. I knew that, despite being on vacation, however, I could not stop my physical therapy exercises each day or my struggle to heal and gain weight.

I was depressed to be told by the Physical Therapist that it would be another three months before I could drive, manage stairs easily, or ride a bike. I had not yet achieved a ninety-degree range of mobility in my legs. Although I had the beach in my future, I dreaded a summer of prison ahead, still dependent upon others. I wanted a strong man to give me a hug and reassure me that everything would be all right. As always when upset, I withdrew to my inner self to find comfort. I saw no reason to inflict my sorrow on anyone else. I tried to cry silently at night so that my mother would not hear me, and I wrote reams of despair into my journal. Would I ever have a pain-free hour or day or week again? Could I really manage my life and those of my children on my own again? When would I be able to work? What sort of work could I do? Would I ever stop being ugly? My life was in two separate realms—a public facade filled with cheer, as the brave victim helping normal people bear my suffering, and a private world overflowing with sorrow within my lonely self. I wanted to know how long all this would last. I longed for a normal, fun life again.

Slowly the swelling receded and my new mouth healed, as I persisted with my Brecht feeders. I hated wearing a towel pinned around my neck. I would not go anywhere, fearing stares of revulsion. I was glad I had such a large collection of hand-me-down towels from Mum. I used one every few hours, drooling in the summer heat. Each time I bent over, drool flowed out of my mouth. I learned to keep my head up and to one side washing my hands, so that they were not slimy with drool. Drying them had to be above mouth level. Every day, I would try to bend my legs to reach my very own shoes and socks all by myself like a Big Girl. My feet seemed worlds away. I was anxious and kept trying, though it seemed an insurmountable mountain. One day I surprised myself and actually got a foot into a sock. I rang my bell in triumph for Mum, who came running, afraid that a catastrophe had happened. "Look what I can do!" I waved my proudly clad foot at her. We laughed together, more excited than we were with my First Step or First Bite.

Next, Mum and I went back to the University of Virginia to have my legs checked and x-rayed in Orthopedics. The doctors felt I was progressing well, although I still wanted instant improvement. In the Craniofacial Clinic, Dr. Chuong was happy with my jaw's healing. Dr. Lambruschi joked, "No one will ask you for a date unless you get that packing out of your mouth, Gari." I knew I still had to endure it and did not think he was funny. Dr. Chuong swiftly pulled out the packing and plastic splints, making my mouth feel empty, despite all the wires threading through my gums and teeth. He checked the positioning of the jaw and put the splints back until my fall checkup. I wanted it all to be over. Patience was a hard lesson for me.

Mum and I got Tom ready for camp, compiling all the clothes and equipment listed. Next it was my turn. Clothes were a problem, because I still had not gained back the lost weight. Everything sagged on me. My shop manager came to my rescue, with several loose dresses which concealed my gauntness. Most shoes hurt my feet. I was comfortable only in slippers or sandals. Now I could commiserate with Chinese ladies, whose feet had been bound and who could not walk. I had existed in nightgowns and slippers for so long that I had forgotten what it felt like to wear Real People Clothes.

Tom was awake at the crack of dawn on the day of the drive to Baltimore. He came down to see if I thought that his Grannie would ever wake up. In a short amount of time, we all had breakfast, got dressed, and, when the car was packed, took off. I felt a thrill to ride, for the first time, in a car for fun instead of going to surgery or doctors' appointments.

I quickly found that my new voice did not carry in a car because of traffic noise. No one could hear a word I said. It was futile to try to take part in conversations. I needed my Magic Slate. Even though we were just sitting, I was not used to being up for three hours. When we passed the location of the accident, Tom pointed it out. The guard rail was still mangled. I felt strangely removed from it, as if I were looking at an historical marker. It seemed hard to believe all that had happened in that spot, which now looked rather innocent. Later, on the Interstate, we stopped briefly at a rest stop. Mum helped me into the ladies' room, glaring at all who dared stare at me, as I drooled into my towel. I thought what a freedom it would be to look normal enough so that no one would stare at me. My priorities had changed from enjoying being the center of attention to longing to be able to secretly blend into the crowd.

As we drove up to her house, my stepmother came out to greet us and help with bags. Tom and his two grandmothers managed the luggage while I hobbled on my crutches. It seemed strange not to be the one carrying things for everyone else. Mum hugged and kissed us goodbye and left to return to her own house.

The next morning, Tom was up early again, ready to leave on his camping adventure. He felt that everything took forever again. We drove him to the airport, located the camp group, and tagged his luggage properly. Tom was wonderfully unembarrassed having a mother who drooled. We waved at the group on their flight and drove back to get ourselves and the dog ready. After many years, I was excited to return to the beach cottage where I had spent much of my childhood. The drive was smooth and easy. The house looked very different because of reconstruction due to a major hurricane. I promised myself, "If this house can be smashed and rebuilt, so can I. I will look just as terrific as it does when I am done."

My stepmother brought all sorts of new soup recipes to cook for me while we were there. I was hopeful that I could finally gain some weight to pass the 85-pound mark. It was delicious having a change of menu and breathing the salt air. I sat on the deck watching the waves and felt the salt wind heal my mangled face. I relished the smells and sounds of the ocean and its shore birds.

My half-brothers came to visit at the beach while I was there. It was the first time we had seen each other since my accident. They were marvelous about not looking at me with horror, despite my drooling raw-hamburger-like face. One of them, an artist, was fascinated at how the bones were being reconstructed. He asked if he might touch my face to feel what had been done. I was afraid of being hurt but agreed if he would be careful. He was wonderfully gentle, visualizing what had been moved around under the skin from my first face to make the second. He said,

"Anatomy class never seemed as real as your face does. I remember what your first one looked like. I'm impressed at the symmetrical foundation for your second face they have made, considering what was left. It's amazing how it will be similar, but narrower and different."

One day, my stepmother and I decided to go for a walk on the beach with her dog. I wanted to recreate my favorite beach memory of walks as a child. My stepmother felt that, if I leaned on her, I could probably walk on the sand without my crutches. By then, I could use just one crutch though my balance was shaky. Leaving the crutches on the front porch, we started off. The feel of the sand under my bare feet was a wonderful reminder of all my past enjoyment. I longed for independence to come again. We had not walked far when suddenly my best leg plunged into a deep hidden hole from a sand castle. My severed leg twisted under me alarmingly, and I cried out with pain. What a helpless feeling to be trapped! I was not agile enough to get my leg out of the hole by myself. I was immobilized with surprise and hurt. I wept, terrified that I had broken my fragile body again. My stepmother matter-of-factly held my arms and told me, "Take deep breaths, sit down, and try to relax." Meanwhile, she frantically thought of how she could get me back to the house in one piece. The dog circled us, worried. Slowly I calmed down, stopped crying, and realized that the leg could not break again from just falling into a hole. Despite the sharp pains and my fear, together we managed to pull my leg free. Other people walking on the beach stopped to ask if we needed help. My stepmother said, "We can manage, thank you," and we did. She held me up while we stood for a few minutes waiting for the pain to leave. She pleaded, "Please don't tell your mother that this happened, Gari; she will never forgive me."

I laughed. "Don't worry, it is our secret." Slowly, followed by the dog, we limped back to the house, which seemed miles away. I lay down on the deck with my foot up. The next day, the swelling was minimal, and I was relieved to be just stiff and not re-broken.

The rest of the time at the beach passed in a flash, as vacations seem to do—reading, talking, sitting on the deck, and watching the ocean. Mum picked me up and took me back home to Virginia. I felt rested and refreshed after my first change of scenery in six months, and it helped my mother to have a break from dealing with the concerns of her second-time infant. We returned resolved to have me able to manage on my own as soon as possible. I had graduated from the nurse stage, but still could not drive and had no car. We decided that I needed a housekeeper in the interim, until I could walk alone and drive again.

Luckily, Sally, a friend of mine, was looking for a part-time job and agreed to help me out for a few hours each day. I was glad to have a friend with me and not some new stranger, to whom I would have to explain everything. I was reminded of the quote by Richard Bach from *Illusions*: "Your friends will know you better in the first minute you meet them, than your acquaintances will know you in a thousand years." What a gift Sally was to me—she came in every afternoon so Mum could show her the ropes. After Mum went home, she was my lifeline to the world, driving me to doctors and dentists, cooking, gardening, and organizing my life in many thoughtful ways.

I was still concerned about my faulty memory. How could I survive in the real world or work again without it? I was given no "mental therapy" lessons like Physical Therapy. It bothered me to be told to wait by the neurologist. I wanted to do more to make me better. Two dear friends suggested playing cards. They patiently retaught me to play Hearts, Old Maid, and other simple children's games. I found my memory improving by millimeters each time we played. I was finally enjoying improving my mind.

Soon, Tom arrived home from camp, full of exciting stories. I was glad that he had been away from his child-again mother to have fun and not be seriously dependable all the time. Shortly after, Mum and Sally took me to have my plastic splints and wires removed. I tensed up my body to endure the pain to come, but Dr. Chuong gently slipped out the splints. Next he snapped all the wires into small pieces with pliers. When he pulled the wires out of my jaw, it did not hurt, though it did bleed, which worried me. He used a special type of metal to which skin tissue does not stick. I was grateful for his thoughtfulness, as it took two hours to remove it all. Afterwards, I felt shaky and discouraged that my mouth was still drooling. I asked Dr. Chuong again when I would stop. Again he shook his head that he did not know. The grafted gums would always be a weird-looking white, due to the type of skin used. He was pleased that it had all healed in well. I could now put away the Brecht feeders and begin to eat soft foods carefully. I was to start rinsing my mouth with salt water each day to strengthen the new tissue, and, in a few weeks when it was better healed, I could finally start having real teeth made!

When we arrived home, I shut myself in the bathroom. I examined myself in the mirror. Realistically, I was incredibly ugly. The drooling made it worse. Self-pity is such a bore and a cancer as it grows. The doctors said it might take six months for the anesthesia to wear off. Then, I might feel energetic again. I still felt yucky and looked worse. I hated the dullness of healing. I detested people's reactions to my deformities. I avoided facing anyone. It was difficult to keep a smile on my face, when I was weeping with self-pity inside. Would this dreadful time ever end? I must somehow continue to transform my destruction and reconstruction into an enjoyable challenge. How could I do that with my current face?

Soon it was time for teeth to be started. I looked forward to being able to eat Real People Food and bite an apple or an ear of corn again. I was unaware of all the agony ahead to have a normal-looking mouth. Dr. Robert Zachman, who had been my dentist for years, came to the house shortly after I was out of the hospital, to see if there were anything he could do to help out my mouth in the interim. At that stage, he told me sadly, he could do nothing until the jaws were in place.

Mum took me to Dr. Zachman's office and waited while he examined my mouth. It was hard for me to open my mouth very wide for a long period, as it was still sore from the surgery. I did not have a large opening without lips. He was encouraged that the gum tissue or sulcus had healed well, and he liked the way the jaws had settled in. He had consulted with Dr. Chuong to plan a mouth similar to my first one. Due to the bone which was available, the new palate was narrower and taller that the first. The teeth would have to fit in a smaller space than the first ones had. Dr. Zachman asked me again if I wanted to go to a specialist in a big city, but I liked and trusted him. Also, I did not have the stamina to deal with a dentist in a far-away location, with travel and lack of familiarity. I felt more fragile with new people. Dr. Zachman checked his schedule and made appointments for me the entire following week at 10:00 A.M. for the whole day. He said he could schedule his other patients before me. My mouth was the biggest job he had tackled. He felt he should do it in bridges, two on the top and one on the bottom, because of the torque. Mum and I asked about having implants, but Dr. Zachman said that they had not been perfected. I realized that he would have to drill down the teeth which were left to put on the bridges, but, with Xylocaine, it should not be too painful.

The following Monday morning, Mum delivered me to Dr. Zachman's office and promised to be back at 5:00 P.M. to pick me up. As I settled into his chair, which was more padded than the one at the University

Hospital, he adjusted the neckrest to make me comfortable. He thoughtfully painted my gums with a topical anesthetic to numb them so I would not feel the needle going in. His technician held my hand a few minutes later, when the Xylocaine was injected. It was easier than I remembered from the last dentist. I thought that I could just meditate while he was drilling. A friend had told me, years ago, when he had caps put on his teeth, that he visualized floating above the dentist's chair on a fluffy cloud. Now would be a good time for me to try.

First, Dr. Zachman took photos of my mouth from all sorts of angles. Since the work was complicated, he wanted to have good records of each stage. As I could not open my mouth by myself easily, he had the technician hold it with clamps in the positions needed for his photos. By then the Xylocaine was working, he got his drill, and we began. The steering wheel, smashing repeatedly into my face, had demolished half of my teeth and the majority of my jaw. It was sad to think that my few perfectly good teeth which remained had to be sacrificed to help out the areas without teeth; but it was a necessary evil for the sake of looking and functioning normally again. At first, I was able to relax and imagine myself lying on my fluffy cloud. I soon became bored and tried to meditate but could not concentrate. This was just like the time after the accident, when I could not immerse myself in books to escape. I felt terrified to be imprisoned in this position with my body vibrating from the jackhammer-like drilling. Every hour or so, Dr. Zachman would stop for a short break. Then I could close my mouth and he could rest his hands. Periodically, the Xylocaine would have to be renewed as it wore off. I asked to look at the remains of my teeth in a mirror. I was horrified to see that underneath a beautiful white tooth was an ugly narrow black stump. At the end of the day, he put a temporary plastic bridge on the teeth he had ground down. I was filled with relief when Mum picked me up at five o'clock. All I could do was collapse in bed at home.

That evening, when I ate my first bite of dinner, it tasted strange in my mouth. I went to the sink to spit it out. I was revolted to see a bloody mass. I cried as I wondered if life would ever be fun again. Everything hurt and made me cry. Mum and Tom put their arms around me to console me. No hugs could erase my blood or despair. I would have to return to the hated Brecht feeders until the teeth were done. I gave up on dinner and went to bed with my cat and dog snuggled around me.

On Tuesday, it was not as easy to go cheerfully into the office and sit all day again in the same chair of torture. I had no choice. Dr. Zachman gave me a hug and tried to make it as comfortable as possible for me. He explained, "When a doctor knows he is going to hurt a patient by what he does, he has to remove himself and think of the improvement and not the current pain." It was a long day for me—much longer and more difficult to bear than Monday. I asked if we could stagger days, but he said, "Once the job is started, it has to be completed so that the molds can be taken and the tooth construction can begin." The teeth were to be made by a laboratory in Charlottesville, which had made many movie stars' teeth. I hoped they would make me gorgeous and prevent drooling.

On Wednesday it was even harder for me to drag myself to another day of interminable torture. Mum said, "Think of how you'll look with that terrific smile again." and drove me off to my doom. We started off with the same routine. It was all too familiar by now to me. I was impressed by the way that Dr. Zachman tried to keep me cheerful, by reporting our progress and how well he felt I was doing. By then we were almost halfway through decimating my poor mouth. I thought it must be hard for him to have one patient day after day, instead of a kaleidoscope of people with different things to discuss.

Halfway through the day, the Xylocaine wore off sooner than usual. The drill suddenly hit a nerve, stabbing me with a bolt of pain and making me cry. Dr. Zachman immediately stopped, realizing that I needed more Xylocaine. I could not stop crying long enough to confirm it. He sat quietly.

I tried dutifully to control my crying and breathing, but I became more and more hysterical with each sob. Putting a box of Kleenex on my lap, he said kindly, "I'll go out and give you some time to yourself, Gari. Call me if you need me." He and his technician left and shut the door.

Then I really cried uncontrollably, for the first time since the accident. I could not catch my breath. I could not stop. I hated the hideous noises I made. I wondered, "Why me? What did I ever do to deserve this torture? Life was not fair at all!" I sobbed for all the pain and for the ugliness. I sobbed for the nasty stares from people and for the looks of horror. I sobbed for not being able to walk easily and for not eating real food. I sobbed for all I had lost in that tragical instant. I wondered if the room were soundproof. I did not care who heard me. I had to scream out all the agony scrunched up inside me. I was fed up with trying not to upset others—I had all the right in the world to be upset for what had happened to me. I mourned what my poor mouth was losing in this room.

Slowly I realized that I was surrounded by caring people. Everything really had to be all right in the future. My breathing slowed. I made myself stop crying. I called to Dr. Zachman, "You all can come back in—I am ready to go again."

He said as he came in, "Your reaction is like a concentration camp survivor, who is tough throughout the ordeal but breaks down later over a tiny incident. You must not feel bad about yourself for crying. Many patients cry over much less than you have been through." I felt consoled by his understanding words—able to accept my weaknesses in that light.

I wished that we could cancel the rest of the day and I could go home, but that was not to be.

Thursday was not nearly as bad as Wednesday. I felt as if I were reporting to a job I hated and would like to change. On Friday the last tooth was done, a major landmark. Next, all the temporary bridges came off, and a squishy material was put into my mouth to take impressions of my stumps and jaws. After the impressions, I was fitted with new temporary teeth, which Dr. Zachman had molded himself for me. Temporary teeth are fluorescent plastic—so white that they would be the envy of any toothpaste ad—but at least I could see what my new mouth would look like when I was a real person again. Wonder of all wonders, the drooling was slowed down at last, due to the lurid white teeth holding in saliva. I was always on guard to prevent the possibility of drooling, however; I swallowed often and constantly kept my chin up, literally and figuratively. I was happy to do anything to prevent the hated drooling. Dr. Zachman tried to make the new temps as comfortable as possible, but they were bulky foreign objects going into a mouth which was still trying to heal from the last surgery. My wretched mouth felt invaded against its will once again, but I was encouraged to finally be on the road to appearing normal.

When I got home, Mum asked, "What do you want to eat for your first real-food meal?" My mouth was dreadfully uncomfortable. The idea of food, which had been tantalizing for so long, was last in my list of priorities, but I could not bear to use the Brecht feeder one instant more than necessary. We ended up deciding on mashed potatoes, applesauce, and a soft hamburger so I would not have to chew very hard. Dr. Zachman cautioned me that temporary teeth were not very strong, so I should eat only softish foods. How ironic to long to bite into an apple or an ear of corn and have such a boring first meal! As soon as I felt the real texture of the hamburger in my mouth, my eyes swam and filled with tears—I was at another milestone. I discovered a new problem with the first bite. My original mouth had a wide, flat palate and the new one a narrow high arched roof. Food flew up to the top of my mouth and stuck like glue. I tried to dislodge the bite of hamburger with my tongue, gave up and had to pry it out with a spoon. I had no idea that eating could be that complicated. I soon found that if I always took ladylike bites, there was less chance of food sticking to my palate. Since I could not chew very well, food would easily choke me if I took too large a bite. My children adored teasing me about taking rude bites. My new mouth always betrayed me. I had difficulty aiming at my mouth with a fork, expecting the original size and place of my mouth. Now it was narrower and higher up, so I hit my cheek with bites of food. Since I had fleeting sensation in my face, I never knew if food particles were left there. I learned to wipe my mouth after each bite. My children loved telling me, "Wipe your mouth, Mummy," in a turnaround for the years when I had corrected them. I practiced eating in front of a mirror to compensate for my lack of sensation.

Susan, the Physical Therapist, was a wealth of helpful hints to make my life easier. I had trouble drinking from a glass or cup, for example, due to a lack of feeling around my mouth. I poured many glasses of water down my chin before I thought to ask Susan. She said to put the glass close to my lips, then stick out my tongue to touch and guide the glass into my mouth. She helped me practice in front of a mirror until I could do it without other people seeing what I was doing. Such a simple solution to solve my problem and make life smoother! I wondered what it would feel like to kiss a man again.

There was a wait of several weeks before the next stage of the teeth arrived to try. I went in to see Dr. Zachman all excited about seeing my real teeth in my mouth. They looked like a James Bond movie character—they were silver! I must have had an amazed expression on my face as Dr. Zachman explained that the base of the teeth has to be metal for strength. Mine were made of palladium alloy. This stage was just to try the fit before any porcelain was bonded on. When he had me sit back in the chair and tugged at the temporary teeth, I felt as if he were pulling apart my carefully restructured jaw and held my breath in terror. As he took out the first section, I breathed in through my mouth with relief and almost fainted from the pain. Dr. Zachman had forgotten to tell me that the stumps of my teeth were exposed nerves, very sensitive to any air, temperature change, or touch. I never forgot again to breathe only through my nose when any work was being done in my mouth. Later, I learned to avoid any hot or cold food or liquid, as metal conducts temperatures more rapidly than real teeth. He took out the other sections of temporary teeth, gently cleaned the sad stumps and carefully inserted the silver teeth. They felt huge and lumpy and uncomfortable. I remembered that a Bionic Woman is never the same as a real one. I thought it was going to feel the way my first mouth felt. After Dr. Zachman had me bite on carbon paper to check the fit, looking for discomfort, I asked for a mirror to see what they looked like and laughed. I sure had a silver smile.

The teeth had to be sent back to the lab for adjustment several times before Dr. Zachman was satisfied with the fit. Though he may not have had experience with what I needed, he crafted me a wonderful set of teeth that other dentists would marvel at for years to come. After he was assured that the metal base was the best possible, he sent it to the lab for the porcelain coating. He had me look at all the possible colors for teeth and recommended a color as close as possible to my former teeth. We used the tooth Blair had saved in the Bloomingdale's jewelry box to compare with his tooth chart. I was amazed at the color range of porcelain, like paint chips. I gravitated first to the whitest sample, of course, but he said that in my face it would not look real because it would not match my coloring and I might be sorry later. He had a point and I remembered my disastrous attempt to be a blonde and have more fun when I was sixteen. My mother had hustled me in to have my bright orange hair dyed back to my natural brown color, but it still took a year to grow out. I never tried again to be what I was not, so marshmallow-white teeth were not for me.

Several weeks later, the next stage of teeth was ready. I had to go over to the lab for adjustments made with their equipment. I was fascinated to see pictures of all the stages in making teeth. I did not like having my temporary teeth taken out. I hated having to sit with only the stumps and my mouth firmly closed against air. I was afraid I would forget and open, while I waited for them to do the work necessary on the teeth. I brought a book to read, but found it impossible to concentrate. The owner of the lab sat beside me and told of his accident. He still had many deep scars on his face and told me he just could not cope with another operation after a while. It was easier for him to live with the road map of scars than deal with the pain and disruption of his life again. He took charge of his life and made his own decision for his body. I wondered if I would persevere or decide to stop before the end as he had. I was not sure how much strength was left within my fragile self. Finally, the lab had enough fittings in my mouth, and my temporary day-glow-white plastic teeth were replaced. I could breathe through my mouth again—what an important freedom!

Finally, after an interminable series of weeks of waiting, my teeth arrived at Dr. Zachman's office, to be permanently installed. Dr. Zachman took out my yucky temporary plastic teeth. He said, "I think I will just put the permanent ones in with temporary cement, Gari, in case there are any problems. I can then take them out easily anytime to make adjustments. Later when we're sure they are comfortable, I can glue them in permanently."

I did not want any more time toothless than necessary, but agreed, saying "OK, but I sure hope they do not have to come out again. I have been waiting to bite into my first apple now that I have real teeth again!"

Dr. Zachman explained, "You will have to be very careful biting, as these teeth are smooth and round on the edges. Your first teeth were sharp and pointed. It is impossible to make porcelain teeth cut like real ones. You still have three original teeth in the back on the left and should do all your chewing using them. You will be able to grip and tear gently with these new teeth. Because of the torque, I doubt that you will ever be able to crunch into an apple, but you can eat it cut up."

I was devastated. I had been looking forward to an apple ever since I lost my teeth. No one told me, until now, that I would never again be able to feel that sensuous crunch into the apple skin and the enveloping burst of juice and apple smell. I would never again savor the first puncture bite of an ear of new corn, as the corn and butter mingled in taste and smell on my face.

"No corn on the cob either, I guess," I said.

"I am afraid not—you must also beware of chewing gum, popcorn, or any sticky food or candy like taffy, as well as hard-to-chew foods like steak."

"Being a Bionic Woman certainly involves relearning life. At least I have the memories of all those former pleasures," I said sadly.

Chapter 9

I felt in perpetual limbo as I healed. Days passed as if I were meandering in an unending stream of sameness. I planned many things but finished only a few. I longed to drive again and regain my lost independence. I felt I must sell my house and move to a one-story place where I could get around easily without help. I realized, however, that I would have to heal and recover considerably before I could manage a move. It was dull to rest and recover. My self-pity rose and fell like bread dough, and I guarded against it by setting goals to keep my inner order. I had accumulated possessions for ten years in my house; to give me a project, I could start eliminating for a move, while I healed.

Mum and I decided that she could go home until the next surgery. I would manage with Sally to drive me and run errands. We sadly cried when she left; it felt as if we had reached another major stage in my second growing up. Though I was impatient with dependence, I was not truly ready to be on my own again. I moved myself back upstairs to my very own bedroom, with Sally's help. She arranged for the hospital bed to be removed and restored my dining room to its former state. We turned the table into a desk, where I could spread out to write thank-you notes for flowers and gifts. I owed millions of notes. I was reminded of all those I wrote after being married. How different it was now—then I had been young, full of hope and happiness, with a new life unfolding. Now, I had a new life to begin, but one alone, filled with despair, terror, pain, and vulnerability. I tried to hide this side from the world by my cheerful optimistic smile. I was overwhelmingly grateful for people's help but longed to control my own life again. With fierce determination, I set my little kindergarten goals and made myself write at least four thank-you notes a day. Each one was a triumph, an achievement over another challenge.

My wonderful friend Blair, who had taken my children for the night of the accident, called and invited me to a movie with herself and her husband. I was thrilled, as I adored and missed movies. This would be my First Outing. I was not sure I could bend my leg enough to get into a movie seat, but she felt that if we sat on the aisle I could keep my leg straight. It was a special evening being with them and seeing *King of Hearts*, a funny foreign film with Alan Bates and Genevieve Bujold. It was such a milestone to see a real movie again that it would not have mattered what it was, and I found that it was not scary or difficult getting into the theatre or the seat. Little pleasures, which I formerly took for granted, kept increasing in value to me. I was blessed by all my thoughtful friends, who gently helped me over hurdles to a more normal life.

Sally cooked wonderful meals for us, gradually using up the food in my freezer. I was convinced I would be moving soon. She helped me ease back into real life by putting an order to my chaos in little thoughtful ways, restoring to me the gift of independence. The most exciting of these was my trip with her to look at cars to buy. My main concern was to have a car made out of tough metal, so that I could not be smashed again. I found that this concern limited me to either certain foreign makes or an old American one. We finally found a safe elderly Mercedes 220 diesel sedan, with an automatic transmission, which I could afford. Sally arranged for me to have a handicapped license plate. Though my legs were not flexible enough to drive a stick shift car, I could manage two pedals. I felt as excited as I had getting my driver's license at sixteen or my first very own car after college. It was a goal not only of maturity, but of freedom. I triumphed taking another step toward regaining the control of my life I had lost. We worked together double-time on the physical therapy exercises to strengthen my right gas-pedal/brake leg. Surprisingly, I was not afraid to drive, but I was convinced that all other drivers might speed toward me; this made me alert to any cars near me. Sally slowly coached me on driving; just like walking, I had forgotten all the necessary moves. I felt slower at learning than I had been as a teenager, though just as anxious to have the skills. My son became an opinionated back-seat driver and was my sharpest driving critic. On the road we were an unbeatable team!

One day, while complaining in my journal about hurting due to rainy weather, I decided that I should concentrate on all the good which had happened to me since the accident. I wanted to keep a list where I could read it whenever I became discouraged. I thought that I might find two or three benefits, but the list grew:

1. Instead of feeling unworthy, I felt people cared for me.
2. I had learned to listen and not talk constantly.
3. I knew wonderful people whom I would never have met otherwise.
4. I was getting my house cleaned out and simplified, ready to move.
5. My voice was a lower pitch, as I had always wanted.
6. I had plenty of time to read books I had bought but never opened.
7. I had gained a closer and better relationship with my mother.
8. I had learned how precious it was to breathe and eat normally.
9. I no longer got upset over things I disliked but could not change. I had learned to let go and let God take care of it.

10. I was grateful for my continued closeness with my son and for his reliability when I needed him.

11. I realized how lucky one was to be able to move easily, walking or running.

12. I understood the freedom of being able to drive where one wanted.

13. My relationship with Emily had improved so that we could be friends again.

14. My enzyme deficiency had reversed and I could eat normally.

15. I had gained an appreciation for my dog and cat clustering around to help me heal, showing their understanding of my sorrow, hurt, and weaknesses.

16. I could stand up alone without pain.

17. I had learned to enjoy receiving, instead of always giving.

Thereafter, whenever I wrote unhappily in my journal, I pulled out that list and reread it, to remind myself how lucky I was. I resolved not to allow others to undermine my self-esteem. It was interesting that I did not feel the need to write when I was happy, because those feelings were acceptable to express to anyone else. I wanted to inflict my despair only on my journal. Good manners do cover up true feelings much of the time.

I got Tom to drag the old blackboard down from the attic. We put it on the landing of the front stairs, with a box of pretty colored chalks and my quotation notebook behind it. I copied on it, "What has happened, has happened; What I am going through, I shall rise above; and what will come, I will meet with courage," by the Sufi, Hazrat Inayat Kahn, which Yusuf had recited to me in the hospital. I reread the sentence each time I slowly made my way up or down the stairs. It helped me feel less alone and afraid. Every few days, I put up a new quote for inspiration.

Now that I could manage, I began reading out loud to Tom each night, as I used to do when my children were tiny. We began with *The Secret Garden*, by Frances Hodgson Burnett, the story of Mary, orphaned in India, who is sent to live with an uncle in England and must learn to make friends for the first time in her life. As we read parts we liked, I would copy them on the board to savor later. We each found parallels between Mary's struggles and our own. Each small pleasure, such as sharing reading old favorites, filled me with quickened healing. At times, however, I felt that putting all my broken parts together by tiny kindnesses to myself would take forever.

By now it was October, seven months since the accident. My next hospitalization was waiting for a cancellation in the fall schedule. When I went in for my checkup, Dr. Edgerton was happy with the good healing of the jaw and other bones, and he congratulated me on my new teeth, which he felt were perfect for my face. The problem with drooling was not as intense as before, though sometimes it surprised me and slipped out, so I had learned to keep a linen handkerchief. Dr. Edgerton asked, "What bothers you the most about your face? Which part would you choose to have changed next?"

I was thrilled to have a choice. "The nose—then people won't stare at me with such horror." To prepare for the rhinoplasty, which comes from the Greek word *rhin* for nose, he asked me to bring him photos of my first nose at different angles. Also, I was to look at noses and choose pictures of my favorites, and he would try to make a synthesis of the possibilities for me. This was finally going to be fun—having a part in deciding what my new face was to look like. Of course it would be pretty, like my first one.

I returned home and leafed through the old photo albums. There were several pictures from modeling and others with the family which showed my former nose clearly. I began looking carefully at noses in *Woman's Wear Daily*, which I read to keep abreast of the latest fashions for my shop. I was amazed that some of the loveliest ladies have the world's ugliest noses. I realized that beauty is a total look, not perfection in all parts. I cut out advertisements with noses I liked, and I presented about fifty pictures at my next visit with Dr. Edgerton. When he saw the number of noses from which to choose, he laughed and said, "Gari, do you think you could narrow your choice down to ten? It would make my job easier."

I realized that I would have to be more selective. I said, "What I really want is a nose like my first one. I need a nose which will hold up my glasses, but a little longer and straighter, so that no one can see if my nose is dirty."

Dr. Edgerton agreed. "That will suit your new face very well, since it is longer and a little thinner than your original shape. We can never make you look exactly as you did before, but we can achieve similarities. I was concerned that you would want a nose which did not fit your face. Many people come to see me for 'nose jobs' and want tiny cute noses which do not suit their faces. I do what they want after explaining symmetry and proportion for their shapes. Many times, they return in tears, asking me to restore their original noses. I have to say sadly that it is impossible. For this reason, I want to be sure that I know exactly what you want before we start." I appreciated his honesty and caring. How lucky I was to have such thoughtfulness, as well as technical expertise in my reconstruction! Dr. Edgerton added, "You must remember that the nose filters and cleans the air we breathe, as well as humidifying and preheating it for the throat. A change in the nasal passages will alter the tone and timbre of the voice. The nose is like a tent, so the shape is determined by the framework. It is important that we are both clear on exactly what is possible before we begin."

"Dr. Edgerton, I will be thrilled to breathe again. I know that I'll be happy with whatever nose you construct for me."

The nose was to be made from a section of one of my ribs. I would hurt in two places instead of one. I felt I could only handle a single area of pain—I remembered the agony from the last surgery too well. The only alternative, however, was to make the nose from a plastic splint, which might warp. Every time I caught a cold, there would be a danger of infection, and the plastic nose might have to be removed. I had no intention of going through nose building more than once, so I opted for my rib to be sacrificed. The rib chosen for women is on the right side directly under the breast, to hide the scar. I did not think that my tiny breast could hide anything. The right side is a safer choice, being further from the heart. For someone who was scarless before, I certainly was accumulating them now—from the accident and from using parts of my body to remake others. Beauty certainly has its price. I had it free in my first life, but now I felt I paid a lot and still was not pretty.

Since I was more mobile, Tom wanted me to go with him to a parents' night at Cub Scouts. He would be putting on a slide show about our trip out West the previous summer. He thoughtfully told me, "Don't worry about anyone saying anything nasty about the way you look. If they do, I will smack them in the face."

I smiled, touched at his concern. "Everyone in town knows what happened to me. I really appreciate your offering to defend me. I know we'll be fine together."

The evening was fun, and Tom's slide show was a great success, especially when he showed his favorite slide. He told the audience that they would see him and his sister at the Grand Canyon. The screen showed Tom beside a bored-looking mule, waiting to ride down into the canyon. The other Cub Scouts laughed and clapped; I knew Emily would be indignant when she heard what he had done. I relished being able to do motherly real-world events again with Tom.

While I was awaiting the next surgery date, slowly becoming more independent, I drove alone to Washington for a shoe show. I needed to get the shop as full of stock as possible before my next surgical absence. Although I did not yet enter the shop due to my appearance, I became more active in decision making. I felt I could do this buying trip on my own without Mary. Luckily, I quickly found just what we needed to fill in for the fall. Afterward, I arranged to meet an old friend from college for lunch. Since my first face and identity were gone, I often sought out old friends to reassure myself that I was still accepted, as I had been in my familiar first world. I prepared my friend for the fact that he probably would not recognize me anymore. He looked up as I approached his table in the restaurant, rose, and hugged me, saying, "I would recognize those lovely eyes anywhere. You really are a phoenix rising from the ashes. Beauty and charm are a way of thinking and carrying oneself. Yours still shines all around you. You look softer and more feminine than before, in a terrific new way!" What a marvelous pick-me-up! I felt much more confident about my future. We had a fun lunch catching up on each other's news, and I felt elated as I drove home.

But reality swiftly set in again. I was terrified of the pain to come and dreaded being carved up. Until I healed after the nose surgery, I could not wear glasses and would have to depend on my contact lenses. I felt nervous not having a backup. I was also still mortified by drooling at times, and no doctor could tell me when it would stop. All said that the tissue I had lost around my mouth normally held saliva in and that lips as well as teeth would help control it. Drooling is demeaning to one's sense of self confidence. I just wanted it all to end.

Sally had slowly decreased her time working for me, and I was afraid that I could not survive alone. I felt like a child not quite ready to leave home, not even excited about it. All my life now was hard persistent work, to slowly climb back up to my former level of independence. Every little unknown worried me. Sally kindly suggested that she be on call if I needed her so that I would not feel alone. Tom was a great help. He took over the job of opening the oven door to remove casseroles, so the heat would not sear my raw face, and he carried trash and innumerable packages inside and out without complaints.

At this time, amid all else, my divorce was in the final stages of negotiation. I was concerned about finishing up my surgeries before I lost my hospitalization coverage, not knowing what lay ahead of me. But it could not be rushed; I had to heal sufficiently each time before the next stage of surgery could be started. At times, I felt as if I could never win, no matter what. At least the shop was running smoothly and the children were doing well in school. Aware of the control and influence the mind has over the body, Dr. Edgerton suggested that I might like to talk to a doctor on his staff about dealing with each new part of my face. Dr. Ina Langman, a clinical psychologist, proved to be a guiding light in my life, just when I needed one.

My first appointment with Dr. Langman was an opening into a new world of solutions. I was reminded of Marcel Proust talking about having new eyes, not searching for new landscapes. She had marvelous practical suggestions for me to smooth my life. She put me at ease immediately, asking, "What is most difficult for you to cope with in your life now?"

My answer surprised her. "The telephone, as I can't move fast enough to answer if I'm not nearby. Some calls I don't want to miss and others I would gladly avoid."

She told me, "Get an answering machine and keep it on all the time, with the volume turned up as loud as possible. Then you will be able to hear who the caller is and choose whether or not you want to talk to them." How wonderfully practical and simple a solution! I felt that it was extravagant to buy an answering machine just for me; however, I realized that I needed and deserved that freedom and choice.

She asked, "Have you any change in feelings when you look in a mirror at your face, Gari?" She thought this would be my first concern.

"No," I shook my head. "I still think it can't be me. I was a pretty model. What I see is ugly and scarred. I dread nasty stares. I hate the way people recoil when they look at me. I feel guilty that I've upset them. It hurts my feelings when people don't recognize me. I wish I were plain enough to disappear in a crowd. I always pleased people by my appearance before the accident. When this is over, I have to be pretty again, so I can go back to modeling, run my store, and earn a living."

Dr. Langman gently said, "You must change the way you think when you look into a mirror. It is still you, but it is *You In Transition*. What you see now is a stepping stone to improvement with each surgery. Do you think you could look at your present face that way?" Suddenly, from this new point of view, it made sense. My current face was permissible in my life.

She continued, "Children stare at you because of a primitive fear that the same thing could happen to them. They are afraid if they look away from you, their own faces will change right then to be like yours. Grownups stare because it is not ordinary and they wonder how it happened. They do not necessarily mean to harm or upset you. One day, you will be past the stage of people staring at you for looking unusual. Then you will notice people staring at others and remember how it felt."

My first life had been based on perfect appearances and not what was inside the person. What a lifetime of lessons I was learning in the short space of time since the accident! Dr. Langman had a sensible way of putting my feelings in perspective. She added, "With children, sometimes you can break their fear with a smiling remark. Then they will be able to see the real you inside. With adults, the best solution is to stare back, making them uncomfortable, so they look away. It is not proper in our culture to stare at another person, the way it is in Asia or Europe."

I asked, "What could I do about getting individual

insurance coverage? I am afraid that my divorce will be final before all the surgery is finished. The accident case may be pending for a long time. My shop has never been a source of income. I put all my profits back into it to help it succeed. I'm living on savings and have no other avenues to pay for the rest of my face if I lose insurance coverage."

She advised me, "Usually one can transfer to an individual health policy under the same company or join under another group. Since you own your house, perhaps you can qualify under the Farm Bureau in your county."

I had never thought of that possibility. I had been immersed in despair over the loss of insurance, instead of turning to practical solutions. How lucky I was to have her help me solve my niggling problems, just as I had helped others over the years! Now, when I felt discouraged, I knew that I had help just the way I preferred — advice on ways to do it myself as a grownup. I could prove to myself that I was recovered and in control of my own life. How thoughtful of Dr. Edgerton to realize that I needed counseling to hasten healing! I appreciated it being offered within his department; I was certain that I was not the first of his patients with such needs. I was grateful enough for all the patients in the world!

We discussed my nose-to-be. Dr. Langman reminded me that I would not be able to wear glasses for several months; any pressure or weight might harm the fragile new nose. Also, I would not be able to wear a bra, due to the rib incision under my right breast. I laughed. "I have always had trouble finding bras in my tiny size. I needed one only when I was nursing my children, so I won't miss wearing one."

She was surprised that I had chosen a nose for the next surgery, as she felt it to be the least of my injuries. She told me of a new patient of Dr. Edgerton's who had crashed in a glider accident, with facial injuries similar to mine. I said, "How I would love to meet someone else in the same situation — then I wouldn't feel alone with my problems." She agreed and said she would try to arrange it. He was to come to the hospital for his first evaluation soon.

My card-playing friends invited me to a Halloween party. As Tom was already going to another party with his friends, I was free. I realized that if I wore a mask over my eyes, all the scars would show; my eyes, which were the one pretty part left of my face, would be covered. I just could not face going out in public with more handicaps, so I decided I would refuse the invitation. When I called to explain, however, my friend laughed at me and changed my mind by saying, "Why don't you reverse things in your favor, Gari? If you were a bandit, your eyes would be free and your nose and chin covered with a bandanna." Tom and I were both cowboys. We helped each other put our costumes together, and Tom lent me his best bandanna. We decided that we both looked terrific. After I dropped Tom off at his party, I felt flickers of fear as I drove up alone to mine. I took a deep breath and remembered that the first time of any new experience is the hardest. This was a first time for me going to a party not only as a single person, but also a crippled and scarred one. My friends met me at the door and introduced me to the inventive costumed guests. The hostess, a psychic, was disguised as a witch, and I felt uncreative as I admired birds, cats, devils, ghosts, and a dragon. No one could hear my voice over the party din, but I listened and nodded at conversations. I was at a stage in my teeth construction where I had to eat with the Brecht feeder; I managed to drink champagne with it, and it tasted much better than my usual fare. I surprised myself by having fun, as I made it over another hurdle in my second life.

Two magical events were to make my outlook very positive before the nose surgery, despite my fears of pain and trauma. First, a friend called to tell me that she had heard about some surgery pain-control tapes which helped one recover faster. I'm grateful that she was insistent; otherwise, I never would have pursued the matter. Many well-meaning friends had suggested things to help me, some of which appealed and some of which had not. I had learned to thank them for their concern and to do as I wished afterwards, not feeling obligated to try each suggestion. But in this case, I wrote down the phone number of the Monroe Institute, south of Charlottesville, and promised her I would call.

When I called the Monroe Institute, a cheerful, pleasant voice answered the phone. Helen Warring, the Registrar, said that the Emergency Series tapes would be perfect for my future surgeries. They consisted of a series of four tapes: one for relaxation before surgery, one for the operating room, one for the recovery room, and the last for pain control after surgery. They used the Hemi-Sync® system, which stands for hemispheric synchronization. The system is based on studies since the 1950s of the benefits of balancing the left and right brain hemispheres. The left brain controls logical thought and the right controls creativity, emotion, and intuition. In normal life, the right side of the brain has an idea, which the left side picks up to use in our logical world. For example, the right side will remember a person's face and the left side the person's name. Hemi-Sync gives the listener intense mental blissful states with sound, as one's brain is balanced. The system of Binaural Beat uses the principle of sending separate sound pulses or tones to each ear with stereo headphones. This causes the two sides of the brain to join together to "hear" a third tone, the balance between the two, called Frequency Following Response. Both hemispheres of the brain are then placed into harmony with identical EEG patterns. Hemi-Sync can thus rapidly change different patterns of brain waves into synchronicity. The listener is transported into specific expanded states of consciousness, in this case to heal rapidly and ignore pain. We all have this bliss time in normal life, but usually when we least expect it and for a brief spark of time. The tapes help one sustain the higher level of consciousness needed to creatively survive a physical crisis. It sounded like a magic door opening into freedom from pain, if it really worked. I asked her to please send me a set. I planned to start using them before I returned to the hospital. *[NOTE — The Appendix contains a more technical description from the Monroe Institute.]*

I listened to all the tapes when they arrived. The directions caution you to lie on a bed, remove all possible noises such as the telephone, shut out cats and dogs to prevent them startling you, and, finally, to close your eyes and listen with stereo earphones. The tapes last forty-five minutes and you are to rest a few minutes afterwards to reorient yourself. I did all my preparations and listened to the first, "Pre-Op." I heard lovely surf and Hemi-Sync signals, and I could feel my brain flow into relaxation. My body calmed itself in places where I had not realized I was tense. Robert Monroe's enveloping calm voice guided me through a total body relaxation into sleep. A code is given to help one relax: "From this moment on, whenever you desire to relax and remove all harmful tension and emotion from your mind and body, all you need do is think of the number 10, inhale deeply, and exhale as if you are blowing out a candle." I felt super-powerful and free to have a secret 10 code just for me! I enjoyed these tapes! I felt wonderfully refreshed, jumped up full of energy to conquer the world, and was swept with dizziness. The directions were correct—one needs to rest and reorient oneself. After a few minutes back on the bed, I was clear-headed again. What a gift to feel peaceful and relaxed! I used the "Pre-Op" tapes twice a day to enter a pattern of relaxation. I still doubted that the pain-control tape really would work; but, if not, it was lovely being a relaxed body instead of tightly clenching my pain to myself.

The next amazing event happened the weekend before I returned to the hospital, when my only unmarried friend asked me to join her for dinner. She felt that I needed one fun evening to remember before my next surgery. Tom was with his father, so I met her at a local restaurant near the University of Virginia on Saturday night. When I arrived, I found she had a date; I had thought we would be alone. I hated to be around new people with my noseless, raw-hamburger-looking face. I wanted to leave at once. I felt upset, betrayed, and out of place, but she insisted I stay. Her date turned out to be nice, despite not being alone with her, and we had an interesting conversation during dinner. As we were having dessert, my friend surprised me by saying, "You two have had a wonderful time talking together without me saying a word. This was not the sort of evening I had in mind. I'm going to the ladies room. I shall expect the conversation to include me when I return."

I felt enormous guilt. I was not familiar with the singles' world; I had given the impression that I was trying to steal her date without meaning to or realizing I was. While she was away from the table, her date and I agreed that we would not talk together anymore and that I would leave as soon as I politely could. When she returned, however, she decided to find another man in the restaurant to talk to me. I was mortified. All I wanted to do was get out of there and go home, but I was afraid she would be mad if I left. I did not want to lose my only single female friend. I tried to dissuade her, but she was determined. I stood up and said, "I will take care of it." I did not see anyone I knew at the bar. Suddenly I noticed a nice-looking man in a tweed jacket, seated next to an empty stool. I sat down beside him and said, "Excuse me, but would you please pretend you know me for a few minutes? I am in a really difficult social situation and need help."

He gave me a big smile and said, "Sure, I'd be glad to. What happened?" As I explained my predica-ment, we laughed together. George turned out to be a fascinating man. He was attending a seminar at the University of Virginia for his Denver company and did not know anyone in town. We sat and talked until my friend and her date left. Then I thanked him for rescuing me and went home, knowing that I had to check in the hospital early. He came to visit me in the hospital the next day, concerned that I would be nervous before my surgery. I had forgotten how lovely it is to have an attentive man in one's life. He sent flowers and visited each day until he returned to Denver. He continued calling me long distance, several times a day.

Mum returned to drive me to the University of Virginia Sunday morning. After getting last-minute errands done in a flurry, as if I were a pregnant mother before childbirth, I had my usual bag of hospital essentials ready, this time including my new Monroe Institute Emergency Series tapes and tape player. For once, as I was admitted I did not feel the usual panic with my heart lurching into my throat.

I felt lucky to have a bed by a window again. All the nurses on the floor came by to say hello and kindly admire my teeth and healed face. Since the University of Virginia is a teaching hospital, there are student nurses and medical students assigned to each case. It takes longer to tell one's story many times, but I was glad to do so. How else can anyone learn, except by example as well as by book? I had a cute student nurse this time. I explained what I was going to try to do with the Hemi-Sync tapes, and I asked her to watch me carefully and tell me what she thought. If they worked, I would be thrilled, and if not, I wanted my codeine right away. She laughed and said that I would be interesting to observe. She alerted her supervisor and class about my experiment.

For this surgery, I was assigned a dedicated medical student, in awe of Dr. Edgerton and his work. Mark felt lucky to observe and was interested in my use of the tapes. He had learned that invaluable lesson of putting a patient at ease, not taught in medical schools but crucial for a good doctor. The residents and interns came by to say hello and check me over before the surgery the next morning. I explained about the tapes to all of them. They promised to arrange for my tape player to stay with me until the surgery started and to have it ready for me in the recovery room. Dr. Lambruschi and Dr. John Persing felt the shape and position of all my ribs, to select the best one for their purposes. Then they drew a diagram with indelible magic marker on my chest, where they would remove my rib. I felt as if I were being readied for slaughter, and I was not sure I could ever bear to eat meat again. My "Pre-Op" tape comforted me to sleep.

Monday morning, I awakened early and calmly listened to my "Pre-Op" tape. Mum had made me a sign, taped above my bed, which said "PAIN CONTROL TAPES IN USE—PLEASE DO NOT TOUCH OR TALK TO PATIENT." So far it had worked, but it would be more crucial after the surgery. I felt relaxed, calm, and very hopeful about having a real nose for breathing. The student nurse appeared to take my blood pressure and temperature before and after any medication was given so that she could make a comparison for a talk at her class that afternoon. She was amazed at how my blood pressure and temperature were lowered after listening to my tape, despite not having any medication. She said, "Most patients' vital signs are elevated because of anxiety before surgery." Mark congratulated me on keeping my vital signs low when he appeared. He told me to remember that he would be observing and rooting for me in the operating room. The floor nurse came in to give me preliminary medication, and then Mum arrived and we waited and waited and waited. I was relaxed but not bored listening to my "Pre-Op" tape over and over. Finally, the nurse returned and said that because there had been an emergency surgery mine was to be delayed for several hours. I told Mum to go home, that I would have a nurse call her when I was done. I was relieved that the bed next to mine was empty, giving me privacy and quiet to immerse myself in Hemi-Sync tranquility. I reflected on my former anxiety and was grateful for the gift of this calm oasis. At noon, the orderly arrived for me, and I climbed on the stretcher with my tape player. I switched tapes then to "Intra-Op" and felt wonderfully serene and happy, instead of shivery and queasy as I had in the past. The green doors seemed to welcome me in the Operating Suite this time. I was left in the waiting cubicle, still peaceful with the security of my tapes. The nurse put in the I.V. needle, which did not bother me, to my amazement. I was wheeled into the operating room and slid onto the operating table. Strangely, the same hard, cold metal table did not seem as foreboding as before. I had no need of extra blankets, despite noticing the cold air and extra bright lights all around me. I was no longer terrified! I was warm and secure and in control of myself at long last!

Dr. Edgerton came in the operating room and patted my shoulder, asking, "How are you today, Gari?"

I answered, "I feel much calmer and happier with these tapes."

He smiled. "I am glad they are working for you." He pulled some pictures out of his pocket to look at them and me; I saw that they were ones I had given him, of me and glamorous models from *Woman's Wear Daily*. What a thoughtful and painstaking craftsman he was, to go to such extra trouble over each little detail. Dr. Edgerton smiled again. "Please tell me again exactly what you want for your nose."

"One to hold up my glasses, long and straight like before and the right size for my new face, please," I said.

He laughed. "That's not too difficult a request. I think I know exactly what you want, and I will do my best."

I smiled back at him and said, "Thank you so much for your thoughtfulness, Dr. Edgerton. I know I'll love breathing through a real nose again."

With my children, Emily and Tom, before
the accident. *Courtesy of Tim Brown*

February 27, 1982. After UVA plastic surgeons stitched up my face. The main entry of the steering wheel was through the chin. *Courtesy of Dr. Milton T. Edgerton*

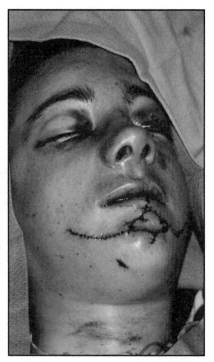

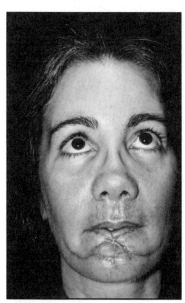

July 1982. Chin, lip scarring, and flattened nose. *Courtesy of Dr. Milton T. Edgerton*

My gifted surgeon, Milton T. Edgerton, M.D. *Courtesy of Dr. Milton T. Edgerton*

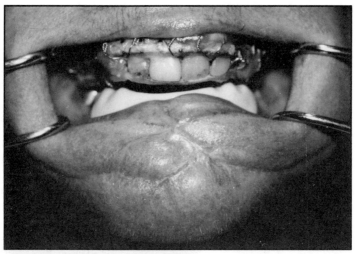

August 1982, show-
ing splints and wires
holding grafted jaws
in place. *Courtesy of
Dr. Milton T. Edgerton*

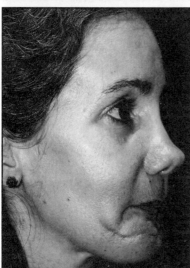

November, 1982.
Side view of new jaw.
*Courtesy of
Dr. Milton T. Edgerton*

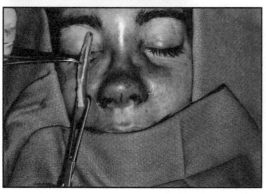

November 1982.
Section of rib
removed to be used
to reconstruct nose.
*Courtesy of
Dr. Milton T. Edgerton*

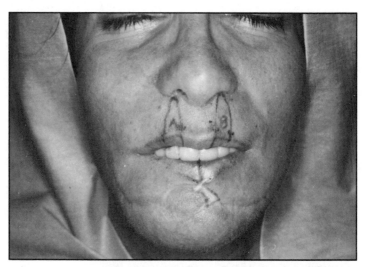

April 1983.
Drawings for
Abbe flap surgery
incisions to graft
lips from palate,
*Courtesy of Dr.
Milton T. Edgerton*

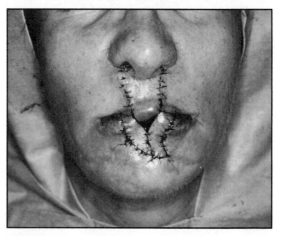

April 1993.
Mouth sewn
together after Abbe
flap surgery for
grafts to grow
together in lip area.
*Courtesy of Dr.
Milton T. Edgerton*

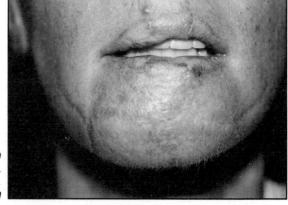

June 1983.
New lip tissue
after grafting.
*Courtesy of Dr.
Milton T. Edgerton*

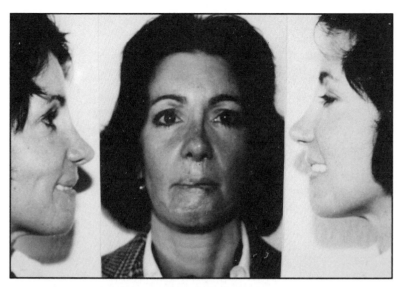

January 1985. View of facial scars and chin taking shape.
Courtesy of Dr. Milton T. Edgerton

January 1985. Pre-operative
view of lip and chin scars.
Courtesy of Dr. Milton T. Edgerton

July 1990. Pre-operative view of
chin scars.
Courtesy of Dr. Milton T. Edgerton

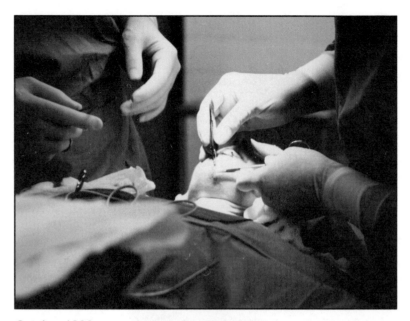

October 1990.
Surgery with Dr.
Edgerton's magic
hands at work.
*Courtesy of
The Monroe In-
stitute—Patti
LeMieux*

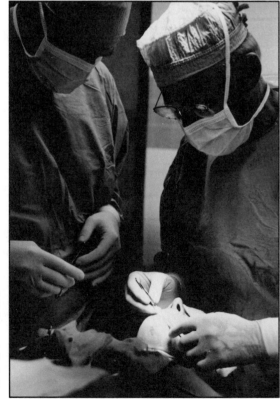

October 1990.
Chin revision
surgery filmed by
The Monroe
Institute.
*Courtesy of The
Monroe Institute—
Patti LeMieux*

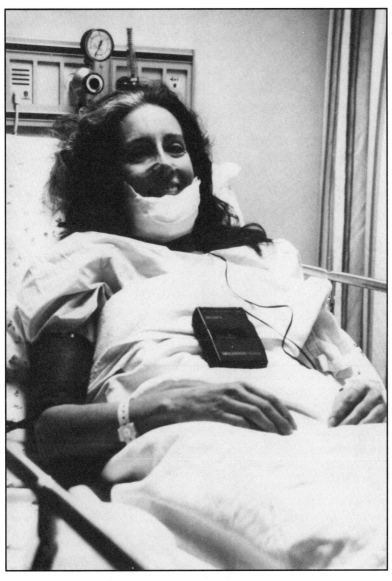

October 1990. Using Monroe tapes in
Recovery Room after surgery.
Courtesy of The Monroe Institute—Patti LeMieux

With my mother, celebrating her 70th birthday. *Courtesy of Susan West*

January 1993. With my children today.
Courtesy of Dr. Steven E. Heyman

The anesthesiologist asked if I was ready to start. I reminded him to please make sure my tapes were there for me in the Recovery Room and said he could begin. The aluminum taste of the anesthesia was not as severe as before. I was quite alert and noticed pain only at a distance, unrelated to me. I remember laughing as the anesthesiologist started jamming his tubes down my throat. Normally I would be gagging, wanting to die at that stage. The "Intra-Op" tape repeats in Robert Monroe's calm trustworthy voice, "You are not alone" over and over. Hearing this made me feel totally supported by the surgical team and the entire world. The surgery lasted four and one-half hours, while they removed my designated rib, closed up that incision, refractured and repaired my sinus cavities, refractured and straightened the bony orbits around my eyes, carved and inserted the rib to make my nose, pulled skin from the sides of the face to cover it, and then, finally, reconstructed nostrils.

As soon as I was alert in the Recovery Room, I was given my "Recovery" tape. I felt relaxed and calm, despite a tightness when I breathed because of the constricting bandages on my chest. I was aware of my exciting new nose being packed and bandaged. Tape ran from ear to ear across my face over gauze. When I gingerly touched my face, I felt a metal frame like the nosepiece of a suit of armor. Mark, the medical student assigned to me, came running in excitedly and exclaimed, "Gari, Gari—watching Dr. Edgerton carve your nose was like watching Michelangelo sculpt a statue! It was such a lovely job of craftsmanship. I felt privileged to be there. I hope that I can be as good a doctor as he is. It was awe-inspiring!" I had not thought before about the rib having to be carved, but of course that made sense. As a layman, I had just thought that they cut the right length and stuffed it in. I had no idea of all the complexity involved. How very lucky I was that someone as skilled as Dr. Edgerton was making my new face!

I felt tired, happy, and calm. I passed the day

resting, listening to the "Pain Control" tape whenever I felt a twinge of pain, and sleeping. There are two versions of this tape; one side is a general guided relaxation and the other, which is my favorite, is called "Energy Walk." In the "Energy Walk," one is transported from the seashore to a grassy meadow to a special favorite tree. I always thought of a beautiful red maple I used to have outside my kitchen window, on a farm where I once lived. I relished each visualization in contrast to my spartan hospital room. The code for pain control is, "When you consciously wish to turn down pain signals from your physical body until they are no longer important, all you need do is: First, look with your closed eyes at that part of your physical body that is the source of such signals; second, as you look, repeat in your mind the number 55515." It worked! I never needed any pain medication after the surgery, which relieved the nurses from paying me extra attention. They were glad and amazed that my experiment was working. Dr. Edgerton was impressed that I had a minimal amount of swelling, had no black eyes or bruising, and healed quickly on my own.

The next morning, Dr. Persing gave orders for my I.V.s to be removed, enabling me to walk around and eat normally. Before, I always had to continue on I.V.s several days, imprisoning and depressing me further. I felt hopeful that I could conquer my world with these tapes. It was such a gift to control my own pain when I needed and not be at the mercy of a codeine shot every four hours. I wished that I could pass on to others this gift of feeling pleasure, gratitude, and joy instead of fear and pain. The future was not nearly as frightening since I had graduated from victim status to harmonious control. Finally, I would be able to see some progress in my face.

The following day, when the residents and interns made their rounds, they complimented me on not using any pain medication and remarked how good I looked. They decided that even though it was only the second day post-operative, after four and a half hours of surgery, my packing could come out because I had healed quickly. Dr. Lambruschi came back after rounds and said he would make the packing removal as easy as possible for me and that I should not be afraid if it bled a little. He carefully peeled off the tape all over my face. I was shivering with anticipation to see my new nose—like a child with a new dress. He gripped the end of the gauze inside one nostril with his gigantically long tweezers. Suddenly, he ran across the room, pulling out of my nose the longest ribbon of gauze I had ever seen in my life. All I could say was,"Oh, Oh, Oh!" as I felt cold air jolt half of my new nose.

He joked, "We like to keep you surprised. If I had done it slowly, it might have hurt you."

I was a little more prepared for the second half—it was almost funny the way he got ready for his race with gauze. How much nicer it is to have doctors joke around with you than to have them proclaim doom and gloom! I was impatient for a mirror, to see how my new face looked with a real nose. He cleaned up the area around the nostrils and looked inside with a light, pleased that it had healed quickly and well. Finally, he produced a mirror from his pocket and said, "You should admire the left nostril more, which I stitched."

I took the small hand mirror and saw the most exciting, beautiful nose in the world sitting on my very own face. The shape was lovely and just long enough to fit in the area. Though still swollen, it looked bony and sparse with skin tightly stretched in place. I asked if I might touch it and did. It felt just as it looked—all rigid bone with no wiggle of cartilage.

Dr. Lambruschi assured me, "That will fill in with time. It has to heal in place, first. I am going to put the metal splint back on it and you must be very careful not to blow it or move it in any way. Here is a bottle of Dr. Edgerton's special nose medicine.

You must put several drops in three times a day to help the interior heal. When you come back for your checkup, we will be able to take the splint off and remove sutures out of your chest. Since the rib area is healing very well, you may be discharged tomorrow, instead of spending a week here as we first thought. I am glad for you that your surgery tapes have made such a difference helping you recover."

The next morning, Mum arrived to take me home in triumph. I was proud that I had tried the tapes and they had worked. Before I left, all the residents told me, "Don't ever walk into a glass door and hurt our nose, Gari. We all worked too hard on it to have it destroyed." What a responsibility to safeguard their nose the rest of my life!

Chapter 10

I felt a shock strike my new nose as we walked out of the hospital. Suddenly, I could smell, in sharp reality, the bitter stench of coal burning from the hospital furnaces' smokestacks. I had forgotten the acrid odor, though I had been past the huge pile of coal many times. I felt just as I did when I first learned to see again—my impressions were sharp daggers, in contrast to the gentle, hazy world of unreality where I had been. The car exhaust around us pierced my throat. I had not missed those hurtful smells at all! I longed for some favorites like roses or cinnamony apple pie baking or a marvelous man's cologne. I knew they were all to come in my new life. Polluted smells were intensely intrusive, unlike delicate pleasurable ones. As we drove home along the winding country road, I wished it were spring, so I could practice smelling newly mown grass or blooming honeysuckle. The dry winter landscape of bare fields with post and rail fences glimmered with stark reality after the sterile hospital room. I was grateful to be out in the real world again, and it was reassuring to be able to walk up my own steps without crutches after this surgery and to be welcomed by Tom and the dog and cat.

Mum felt confident that I could manage healing alone after just a few days and went home. Finally, I was able to see some real progress on my face, despite the splint. I found that I was more comfortable scrunched over like a fetus to protect the rib area. Any stretching or deep breaths pierced the depths of my being with pain.

In a week, I drove proudly all by myself to the Craniofacial Clinic to have the splint and stitches removed. First, I saw Dr. Langman, who reminded me, "You have to adjust to a new self-image, since your face has changed drastically. Stop thinking that you *were* pretty and concentrate on your inner self being pretty *now*. Though the teeth were another loss, you have gained a nose. If you find that people do not recognize you and hurt your feelings, look on it as a stepping stone to a new person, not a stumbling block. You must remember to pace yourself more and not expect to be Wonder Woman."

"Thank you, Dr. Langman," I answered, "for reminding me of all I must learn in this new life! You make each stage clear for me with your wealth of good advice, just when I need it."

When I went into the comforting waiting room, I noticed a young man with a bandaged face similar to mine. The coordinator came in and introduced us; he was the guy from the glider accident, whom Dr. Langman had mentioned.

I smiled and said, "Hello, I'm glad to meet you. My face was crushed just like yours. You're the first person I've encountered in the same situation. I'm a few stages ahead of you in reconstruction. Michelangelo just made my nose. I am sure you'll have just as good a one."

His eyes lit up. "Does Michelangelo really work here?"

I smiled and nodded "yes," as he left to meet Dr. Edgerton for the first time. I felt sorry for him. He had no idea of the length of surgeries and healing ahead of him. I felt light years ahead with my beginnings of a face. I hoped that I had lifted his spirits; I remembered longing for someone who really understood to do the same for me. There was never anyone for me to use as a mentor, anyone who had also lost a face and recovered. What a major leap of progress for me to get to the stage where I could help others again! I felt worthwhile for the first time in my new life.

Next, I was taken into an examining room. I was given the small hand mirror with which each room is equipped, along with the usual medical instruments. Dr. Persing was assigned to me that day. It was fascinating to see, after the splint was peeled off, the tiny doll-like stitches that had been taken down each side of the nose and all around each nostril. As he removed the stitches, the tweezers and scissors felt like tiny flicks of a cosmetic brush against my new nose. In strange, unexpected spots I had feeling which disappeared quickly, like flashes of memory. Next, he removed the bandages over my ribs and the not-so-tiny stitches there. Since I was a small child, I had hated the feel of pulling off adhesive bandages on my skin; therefore, I had been surreptitiously working to loosen the rib bandages. Dr. Persing was not fooled when they came off easily and said, "I was going to ask if you wanted some adhesive remover solution to work with first, Gari, but I see you have been ahead of me again."

Then Dr. Edgerton entered with another resident doctor to inspect my beautiful nose, giving me a big hug. "Gari," he said, "what do you think of yourself now?" It was such a gift for me to have a doctor always concerned about his patient's feelings. He knew that the nose was a major milestone for me in my acceptance of this new face.

I grinned and answered, "Dr. Edgerton, of course I adore it. I promise to take good care of your nose for you. But I'm scared that the bone isn't attached at the top or bottom. It wiggles between my eyes if I touch it. I'm not used to having such a rigid, wobbly nose."

He touched it gently. "That was the only possibility for a nose for you," he explained. "It is a tent made out of your rib. You will always have to be careful. As the swelling goes down, it will gradually fill in on the sides as it heals. We can add bits of cartilage later, if it is not symmetrical, from another donor site, such as the ear."

I did not want to think of any more work being done on my nose so immediately put the suggestion out of my mind. I changed the subject. "Did you hear about the remark by the medical student about your being like Michelangelo when you carved my nose?" He had not, so I told him and we both smiled, knowing how true the remark was.

He asked, "What do you feel when you look in a mirror at yourself?"

I glanced in the hand mirror. "I still feel that it isn't me, because I was pretty and what I see isn't. Dr. Langman said to concentrate on my inner self."

He agreed. "What you see now is your new face in progress. It will improve with each surgery. Trust me."

When I emerged from the clinic into the real world of cold, I felt instinctively as if I should hold a hand in front of my vulnerable nose, the way one holds a hand over a baby's face to protect it. How could I ever fit into the Real World again?

At home, I had to acclimate myself, to protect my new nose as a Bionic Woman. I learned to be cautious putting any clothes over my head, since my rigid nose caught on everything. I could not sleep on my stomach any more, due to the immobile nose, and I found that I had to tip my head way back in order to drink from a narrow-rimmed wine glass, as my nose bumped on the edge. I tried to not flinch when anyone came near to hug me because any bump shoved the floating rib/nose into my skull with a sharp crunch. I learned that only a kiss on the cheek was easy to manage. I also had to support my nose very carefully so as not to scrunch it as I blew it. The new nostrils were narrow, and I was unable to fit a finger with a Kleenex inside to clean them. I had grown up being taught that a lady *never* had a dirty nose. I asked Dr. Edgerton to make me one that no one could see inside. I forgot to say "everyone but me."

All the new veins stood out like red train tracks all over the nose, making me look like an inveterate alcoholic. Slowly, however, they integrated and disappeared. I found that the nose seized my face with pain when I walked outside into the cold. It was even more sensitive than my other broken bones to temperatures and barometric pressures. I was really like a Civil War veteran who could tell when it was going to rain or snow. Unfortunately, there are no coats made for noses. Mum suggested a ski mask, but I could not tolerate the pressure on my scars. I could cover my head, hands, feet—all my body—except for my face from the cold. I learned to walk outside with a glove covering my nose, and I tried to move from one warm place to another as quickly as possible.

Everything seemed to take forever to do by myself. I moved very slowly, so as not to pull any part of my body near the ribs and generally stayed hunched over in order to be more comfortable. I was still taking many vitamins and trying to gain weight. I had reached 100 pounds but seemed unable to get past it. I remembered that I never weighed more than 99 pounds from the time I was sixteen until I discovered how good the food was at Randolph-Macon Woman's College. It is just as hard to lose as to gain weight and just as discouraging without immediate results. I kept busy sorting out my house and visiting with friends who came by to check on me. When I walked my dog each day, I would return to find flowers or food on my front porch, as if Guardian Angels were looking out for me. I felt blessed and encircled by a loving network of casseroles. My maid came to clean and do laundry and help with cooking. Tom was wonderful, making me practice going up and down stairs two-legged like a grownup. Mum called several times a week to make sure we were all right and suggested our going to The Homestead for Christmas that year as we had for the previous five years. She wisely felt it would get my mind off my problems, making me not as aware of being single and deformed. I was thrilled to have something to look forward to and was grateful for her continued thoughtfulness.

Mary felt that I should record some advertisements for the shop to help Christmas sales. I had always done my own radio spots so people would pay attention to a voice distinctly different from the usual announcer. I enjoyed working before a microphone. I was afraid that I would not be as good with this new voice, though ten months had passed since the accident. I knew it was lower in tone and much less strong and I could not speak as quickly or enunciate well, but I agreed to try. Mary and I wrote some copy, mentioning good ideas for Christmas presents which we had in stock. I took it in to the station and tried to hide my nervousness as I sat in front of a mike. My voice trembled as I stumbled over words. I felt discouraged that I had lost another hard-won ability. I always prided myself on having a calm, perfect first take. The station manager, who was acting as engineer for my tape, matter-of-factly asked if I would like to do it over. I nodded, cleared my throat, and began again. The second reading was better, but I had trouble saying all that I needed clearly in twenty-five seconds. As I looked despairingly at the manager, he said that he had plenty of time. He felt that this was something I needed to do to prove to myself that I could be successful. He was right. I took a deep breath, sat up straighter, and began again on cue after two beats of the background music. This time was the best reading, and we decided to use it at prime time for several weeks until Christmas. I was relieved to have another test behind me. I would have to work at my voice to make it better, just like the rest of the new me. The list of my deficiencies requiring attention seemed to lengthen instead of shorten.

Christmas raced upon us. My mother and stepfather drove down from Philadelphia. Mum and I took a cake and presents to the family in the trailer who had helped Tom and me after the accident. Mum remarked while we were there that she felt that if the accident had happened in a big city I would still be trapped in my car. She told the family that we were grateful to have such thoughtful, caring people to help when I needed it. Mum asked about the blankets which they put over me in the car. She offered to replace them, since they were ruined, but was told no. They felt thanked enough by seeing me able to walk into their home alive and well.

Tom, Emily, and I squished into the back of my parents' car for the drive to Hot Springs. Every year, the drive seemed prettier through the big rolling horse farms of the Shenandoah Valley and then across the Skyline Drive, with its lovely vistas, into the Blue Ridge Mountains. As we entered the George Washington National Forest, we followed a sparkling stream down one mountainside on the winding road. The children looked for the bare space where a forest fire had burned trees away years before. Each Christmas a little more had grown back—just like my face, a slow process of regeneration.

There was just enough snow to make it look like Christmas as we arrived at the front entrance of the huge brick Victorian hotel and pulled under the tall white columns of the portico. Along the front of the main building of The Homestead, the old fashioned dark green rocking chairs were waiting on the long veranda. Even though it was cold, some guests were bundled up and rocking. The porters quickly unloaded the car, as we checked in. Mum had thoughtfully reserved rooms in the main building, with a parlor between for presents and extra space. In the main building, I would not have to walk great distances for meals and the children were in the center of all their favorite spots. We went down for afternoon tea in the Great Hall, to listen to the orchestra play old familiar tea dance tunes. There is always the World's Largest Decorated Christmas Tree at the end of the hall, rising to the top of the second-story balcony. It was shimmery blue that year. The children were more interested in cookies than tea or music. The grownups decided to take a nap before the evening reception, while Tom and Emily raced off to see which jigsaw puzzles had been started in the puzzle room, to decide which was their favorite decorated tree in the reception rooms, and, most importantly, to see if any other children they knew were in the game room yet.

Our tradition of Christmas at The Homestead had begun the first Christmas that I had my shop. I had realized that there was no way I could work all those extra hours and still manage Santa and Christmas, so I had suggested that we give each other the present of a trip to The Homestead and just have little stocking presents. Everyone thought it was a super idea. My parents joined us, and we all enjoyed a lovely rest with wonderful food. The trip became a family tradition, as it had for many others over the years.

That evening, we all dressed for the Christmas Eve Reception which The Homestead gives for guests. My stepfather helped Tom with his tie, and my mother tied Emily's sash on her long dress. I was glad to fit into an old familiar, comfy, evening dress. I had practiced wearing high heels at home, to look proper with my long dress. I still had difficulty balancing even in flat shoes. I felt like a young girl with her first pair of high heels. I told everyone I would have to walk slowly and to please stay near me in case I began to fall. Mum wore a pretty new floral dress from my shop and my stepfather wore his dinner jacket. We felt we looked rather smashing as we swept down the hall to the ballroom. As we made our grand entrance, the children gasped in awe at that year's ice sculpture. They had been guessing all along what it would be. The chef had outdone himself and had created a life-sized Santa in a sleigh pulled by slightly smaller-than-life reindeer on the central buffet table, lit with colored lights. Tom made a beeline for the shrimp and caviar. Emily stayed with me, looking around at the other pretty dresses. She pointed out a Scotsman in his kilt and dinner jacket and several ladies with lavishly beaded evening dresses. She was adept at guiding me as I tottered through the crowd, knowing that I was terrified of my nose or body being jostled. I suddenly realized that she had replaced me as the pathfinder in crowds. We slowly wandered from table to table, sampling all the delicacies, which seemed fancier each year. I chose carefully what I ate from the buffet, since I could no longer bite, plus would not feel any food dribbling down my chin. I wiped my mouth often and limited myself to small, easily swallowed treats. I remembered the former enjoyment of crunching raw broccoli or carrots and taking a huge bite of a roast beef sandwich with the tang of horseradish. I kept telling the children to save some room for dinner, which was directly after this reception, but they forgot as they did every year. We had a lovely dinner afterwards, even though the children wanted only dessert. We all danced between courses, Tom and my stepfather doing double duty. As Tom and I slowly did the box step together, the orchestra played *What A Difference A Day Made*. We looked at each other, thinking not of love but of the fateful day in our lives. When we returned to our rooms, all our beds were turned down as usual. On the children's beds were stuffed stockings and a special present for each from The Homestead. They looked forward to this each year. I was grateful to Mum for helping to continue the tradition while I was in transition.

The next morning, we opened presents in the parlor before going down for breakfast with gifts for the staff. It was pleasant looking around the enormous dining room at all the generations of families there every year. I felt incomplete as a single woman and wondered when I would get used to being an unmarried, non-pretty person. As was my face, being single was another major adjustment, after twenty years of marriage. The rest of the vacation passed all too soon. As we left, thanking everyone who had helped us, I wondered where I would be the following year and what I would look like.

After I was back home into reality, my attorney called to say that my divorce agreement was ready to sign after a year and a half of negotiation. Soon after, George, the man from Denver who had continued calling me regularly, surprised me by asking me to marry him on the phone one night. I protested, saying that my next surgery was to have my mouth sewn together. He countered that he had always wanted a wife who could not talk back. He said that he had decided to marry me the moment I asked him for help in my "difficult social situation." He wanted to help me heal under his "umbrella of love." I thought how crazy this was, as we never really had a "date" and knew each other only from talking on the phone. However, he had shown himself to be a kind and thoughtful person, who could see past my disfigurements, and I did not want to spend the rest of my life alone. I talked to Tom and asked how he would feel about my marrying again and moving to Denver.

Tom's face lit up. "I've felt like a tiny flower trying to bloom in a desert against terrible odds. Now the flower will be transplanted in the middle of a beautiful healthy garden." I was amazed at his youthful insight. We hugged each other, realizing that this could turn our lives around to forget the tragedy of the past. I called back and accepted George's proposal.

I called Mum to tell her my news and was met by a long silence at the other end of the phone. I asked, "Are you still there?"

She said, "You had a lot of head injuries in your accident, dear; you really do not know what you're doing. I'll call you back." It takes a lot to make my mother speechless. When she did call back a few hours later, she first tried to make me see the reality of what I was doing, then gave up and said that she and my stepfather would be there for the wedding and wished me well. I thought she was being overly cautious, but I ran into the same reaction from everyone else I told.

One of my closest friends, who had talked to me

about having to learn to accept from others, said, "I won't waste my time trying to talk you out of marrying your Rebound Person. I see you're determined, Gari. Just remember, I'm your friend no matter what happens. I only want the best for you." I thanked him and was grateful that at least one friend respected my wishes.

The next week flew by, as I found a dress, arranged for a small family wedding in my house, sent invitations for a surprise party after the wedding for friends in town (it was a surprise for everyone but me) and arranged our move to Colorado. As people received their invitations, they called my shop to find out the background. Mary told everyone to say she was not there so that she would be able to work. She smilingly said, "You all better know nothing also, or the phone will ring more than it did the day after Gari's accident."

My life was changing supersonically. When I talked to Dr. Langman, she was marvelously non-judgmental. She brought up potential problems of a new marriage while I was still going through reconstruction. I told her that I felt I would be cared for and therefore could bear anything. The knowledge of having that support, rather than an empty life surrounded by possessions, was very important to me then. She asked if I felt ready to be hurt emotionally, as that was always a risk with love. Infatuated, I could not imagine life with George without his "umbrella of love."

I next met the speech pathologist for the first time. We discussed the problems I had encountered recording the ad for the shop. He told me that testing showed that my right vocal chord might be adhered and that I would need about two years of speech therapy to achieve more volume and tone. Overall, however, there could not be much change from my present voice. We made a videotape, to watch my face movements as I talked, and I was given exercises to strengthen my weak facial muscles. I was to remember to open my mouth more, keep my head up, and breathe from my diaphragm. It seemed as if I had a million visits and errands to do before I could be a married woman again. I felt torn by all the commotion and urgency, but I knew that I had to finish and tie up all loose ends before my new life of peace and love could begin.

The sky was a glory of red, gold, and purple when I awoke the day before the wedding. I wondered what it meant for my future. I had no time to think about it due to the commotion of the arrivals of my parents and George with his four children, parents, and sister. We all had dinner together for the families to meet for the first time. George's family was kind and accepting of me, though as surprised as my family was by the news. Tom and Emily enjoyed the other children — two boys, fourteen and ten, and twin girls who were eight, all very good-looking, blue-eyed blondes.

The next day was a turmoil of children. It took several hours of bedlam to get everyone clean and dressed for the wedding and party. By the time I got to the shower, there was no hot water. Then, as I was putting on my dress, my stepmother and half-brother arrived and went up through the midst of my privacy to the attic to borrow my crib. I felt deprived of space and privacy. I would never plan a wedding and party in my own house again. I focused on remembering that it was a happy miasma and a welcome change from solitary healing.

The ceremony was brief, with all the children participating. We barely had time for pieces of cake before guests began to arrive. The whole town had accepted their invitations; everyone was curious to meet this man from Denver who had fallen in love with me when I was disfigured. We stood at the front door to greet guests, who kept telling me it was the biggest excitement in town for years. I was touched by the caring shown by friends, who were glad to see some happiness in my life after so much pain and suffering. For the party, instead of another cake, I had brie cheese baked in puff pastry with sculpted roses, as well as the usual Virginia hors d'oeuvres of ham biscuits, turkey, roast beef, cheeses, paté, and dips.

The next day, after all the parents left, George and I took the children to see Monticello, Thomas Jefferson's house in Charlottesville. My throat burned and my voice became fainter and fainter, trying to be heard over the noise of children's squabbles; I was tired and hurt and wanted my own space of peace back. Next, we drove to Washington and toured the Smithsonian before we flew out. We were all on the same flight to Chicago, where my new stepchildren were picked up by their mother. Then Tom, Molly the cat, my new husband, and I continued to Denver. We arrived in the middle of a huge snowstorm, and my broken bones ached with unhappiness at the climate change. George bravely drove through the deep snow to his condominium, where we would live until I found a house. It was small—with two bedrooms—but adequate for us. Despite the trials of the previous few days, Tom and I relished feeling part of a family again.

I entered Tom in a school which he loved and started house-hunting and learning my way around Denver. I put my Virginia house on the market and called the shop several times a week, arranging to fly back each month for consultations. The dry climate slowly eased my pain and my bones did not click as much when I walked. I found George to be wonderfully patient, supporting me for balance and reminding me "Left foot, right foot" as we walked down stairs; I was not afraid of falling with someone to hold onto. I saw everything in my world colored with eyes of love. Tom adored having a man with whom to enjoy sports. Molly enjoyed prowling around her new territory. Life was good.

One day, after a few weeks of happiness, we had a call that my ten-year-old stepson Charlie was impossible to manage and would have to live with us. I wondered how a mother could not deal with such an attractive, blue-eyed, blonde child. I soon found that Charlie wanted his father's attention constantly. Many conflicts erupted. I began to understand his mother's problems. I realized how easy my own children had been to raise now that I was dealing with an emotionally disturbed child. I started him in counseling. I always had to be on guard, to break up fights he started with Tom or neighbors. I was terrified of my nose being hurt when he started swinging at me. Only his father seemed to be able to handle him when he was in a rage; but George was at work all day, and I was left alone to deal with Charlie. I received several calls each week from his teachers about disruptive behavior and fights. The teachers felt his problems were deep emotionally and would take lengthy counseling to solve. I hoped that counseling would reduce the resentment he felt against me and Tom for taking his father's attention away from him; it was discouraging when he complained to his father over and over that I hated him. I disliked living each day surrounded with strife. The child's aggression was violent and unexpected. He was a real detriment to my own continued physical healing. I had lost my short-lived treasured peace and happiness.

I finally found a house big enough for us and all the children, with a lovely view of the entire front range of the Rockies, to help me heal. It was in a good school district on a quiet cul-de-sac along a Greenbelt, a system of parks running through Denver, which meant that the view from the house would be protected from future building. I flew back to Virginia to pack up my belongings and have them moved to Denver. I was concerned leaving Tom and the cat in a situation that was becoming increasingly violent but was reassured by George that everything would be all right. Mum came down to help me sort things and pack; moving is never easy, but it can be fun if you share it with someone who can joke and help decide which memories to pitch and which to keep. I flew back ahead of the moving van and brought my dog Peggy with me. She had stayed with Emily and her father until I could return for her. Emily told me that Peggy had moped after I left and had even run away. They retrieved her more than a mile from the house, and they had been afraid to tell me, as they knew how much I loved my elderly dog. On the flight she slept on my lap after I pulled her out of her carrier under my seat. I had missed her terribly and worried about her survival in the new household.

The next day, we moved into the new house. I hoped that having more space would smooth things out with Charlie. I got a call from Dr. Edgerton's office that there was a cancellation if I could be there for my next surgery; I had one week to unpack before I had to leave for Virginia again. I hurriedly got the kitchen, bedrooms, and bathrooms functional, working as much as I could each day. I left a mountain of boxes in the living room to deal with later. This time I had my Monroe Emergency Series tapes to use, plus I knew I had a supportive husband at home. Everything had to be all right, if I did not think about Charlie.

Chapter 11

Mum picked me up at the airport in Washington, and we stopped at my shop on the way to the hospital. Mary and Louise had done a wonderful job on all the displays. How I missed the fun of being in the shop each day helping people, arranging clothes, and deciding what we needed to improve the stock! It was not the same from a distance. I wished all my friends were closer. I had forgotten how long it takes to make new ones after moving. For the first year, one has only acquaintances. In my rapid restructuring of my life, I had forgotten how much my support group of friends in town had balanced me before. They would have been invaluable now with the challenges of a disturbed stepson. In my first marriage, I had felt disloyal to complain, so I never confided in my mother. This time, we were friends and I was able to ask her advice. She told me not to get caught in the middle of Charlie's violence, but to step away. She felt that he would lose interest without an audience. Otherwise, she felt he would continue to blame me as he tried to turn his father against me. She quoted an anonymous poem:

> One night in late October
> When I was far from sober,
> I was going to my home with manly pride.
> My feet began to stutter
> And I fell down in the gutter
> And a pig came up and lay down by my side.
> A lady passing by was heard to say
> "You can tell a man who boozes

By the company he chooses."
And the pig got up and slowly walked away.

It became our little private signal. We reminded each other of "The Pig" when either of us felt that the other was about to become involved in a negative controversy. We talked nonstop during the drive, enjoying the luxury of our conversation being free instead of costing long distance rates. I was grateful to my mother for not telling me to give up and come home, despite the fact that she had not approved of the marriage.

When we arrived at the University of Virginia, the nurses admired my nose on the Plastic Surgery Floor. Wonder of wonders, I had a sunset window bed again! Mum left and checked into the Howard Johnson by the hospital, while I used my "Pre-Op" tape to calm down and relax. Dr. Edgerton came by to look me over and was pleased with his nose. He explained, "Tomorrow, we'll take flaps from your palate and attach them to your lip area for grafting. They will have to grow and heal in place for two weeks. We'll leave an opening for you to eat on the side. Later, we'll sever the graft and sculpt your new lips from the joined tissue. The reason for using the palate is that the skin most closely resembles lip coloring and texture and has no hair. We'll also reshape your cheeks and chin to smooth out the scarring."

I asked, "Will I have to go back to using the Brecht feeders to eat again?" He nodded his head, as I said, "Yuck—but it'll be worth it to have lips again. I'm planning to use the Monroe Emergency Series Tapes again, Dr. Edgerton. I'd like to listen to them in the operating room if it might be arranged. I could move the wires from the earphones above my head so they wouldn't be in your way. The only help I would need would be for someone to flip the tapes every forty-five minutes as they end." Dr. Edgerton was interested to see the effect they would have on me in the operating room, and he agreed to do all he could to help me.

I felt comforted and serene, knowing that all would be easier each surgery. I did not miss my former terror in the slightest.

The usual parade of students, interns, and residents came by to examine me and take my history. I was glad that Mum had made me a new sign saying "DO NOT TOUCH OR TALK TO PATIENT WHEN USING PAIN-CONTROL TAPES." It gave me the little bit of privacy I needed to make the tapes work. While Mum was with me, Lee and Blair visited that evening, and we caught up on our lives. Mum enjoyed getting to know my grownup friends; she remarked that she had not known any of them since I was little, due to my moving around.

I was tranquilly grateful for the Monroe tapes after visiting hours were over. Instead of experiencing my old feelings of isolation, terror, queasiness in my solar plexus, and an urgency to get up and run out of the hospital to avoid all the hurt the next day, I was calm and soothed by Robert Monroe's voice telling me to relax. How lovely to have bliss in my life from these tapes, all because I was pushed into it! I fell asleep listening to the "Pre-Op" tape. When I awoke, I used the "Energy Walk" once to remind myself of the codes to relax and delete pain signals. It was easier this time, since I knew what to expect. The unknown is more frightening with pain added. Remembering the end of my father's life, with the pain he endured from cancer, I wished I could have given him the gift of these tapes. Each time I saw him, I felt it would be my worst memory, but the next visit would show more wasting away of his gaunt body. I remember thinking how sad and futile for him to work hard all his life to earn money, when it could not help at all with health. I had been stripped of my good looks, my first husband, and my income, but at least I had regained my health and had wonderful children, a happy married life ahead of me, and an acceptable face to take shape in the future, thanks to Dr. Edgerton. Being able to control my own pain when I wanted, though it took enormous amounts of my concentration, was more important to me now than looks or background or income. My priorities had changed dramatically in the past year, just as my father's had when dying.

The nurse came in to get me ready for my trip to the operating room. I decided to take a tranquilizer as an extra back-up for the tapes. Mum arrived to tell me everything would be all right. This time I knew it would. I put the "Intra-Op" tape into my tape player. When the orderly arrived with the stretcher, it was a relief to be able to say goodbye to Mum and the nurses with a real smile and not a faked trembly one! The trip down to the operating suite was swift and pleasant while I glided along with my tape. By then, I was able to flow in and out of concentration. I could talk to someone and not be jarred into disoriented terror, as I was when first listening. The nurse putting in the I.V. needle asked about the tapes; all medical personnel were interested in the principle. It seemed strange to me that they were not more widely used.

Dr. Persing and the nurse wheeled me into the operating room and helped transfer me onto the table. It was such a delight to be able to do it easily and happily, without pain and icy fear. What a pleasure to remember how dreadful it had been and know that I would never have to endure that again.

Dr. Persing arranged my tape player on the operating table to the left, above my head. He threaded the wires from my ear button speakers under my neck and up the left side of my head. He asked, "Gari, is the sound the right volume? Do you need any changes made, before we start prepping you for the surgery?"

"Everything is fine," I said with a big grin, as they began draping me and sterilizing my face with Betadine.

Dr. Edgerton entered, putting his hand on my shoulder as I opened my eyes and smiled peacefully at him. "How are you today, Gari? Do you remember what we are going to do?"

I nodded. "I'm fine, thanks. How are you today?"

"I'm fine also—thank you for asking. I've assigned a nurse to sit at the head of the table by your tape player and flip the tapes for you every forty-five minutes. You'll not be without them. Remember, we're going to take flaps from the roof of your mouth and attach them to the outside to grow into lips, as well as smooth out areas in your cheeks and chin today. It will be important for you not to move your face or mouth at all as I do this work. I'm going to use a little local anesthesia, so you'll feel a few pricks." I nodded again and smiled. I knew I was in the best possible hands in that operating room, and I also had the best possible voice and Monroe technology to help me actually enjoy the experience.

I drifted off peacefully, with Robert Monroe's voice telling me that I was not alone and everyone was there to help me restore my balance and equalization with healing energy. I could feel a slight pulling and cutting of my face at times, but no pain. I felt no need to open my eyes or move. I felt as if I were having a luxuriously relaxing sleep, totally unaware of time.

Suddenly, I was jarred out of my peace and bliss by the absence of the tape sound. I opened my eyes and saw Dr. Edgerton's face directly over mine as his hands moved around my mouth. I tried blinking my eyes at him, aware that I was not supposed to move my face while he was working on it. He was concentrating intently on the area he was re-crafting and did not notice my blinks. I tried rolling my eyes toward the tape player above my head, to make him realize that it had stopped. Surely the nurse assigned to it would notice. My hands were immobilized, so I could not point. I felt a panicky scream rising in my throat, while I tried frantically to think of what else I could do to get their attention. Finally, I realized I would be able to make a sound without moving my face or mouth.

"Mmm mmm mmm," I said, willing him to understand

what had happened. Dr. Edgerton looked startled, not expecting his patient to be talking back to him on the operating table. His eyes moved to mine and saw that I was staring intently at him and rolling my eyes over to the tape player as I continued to say "Mmm mmm mmm."

He smiled to reassure me and said, "Gari's tape player isn't working properly, she says. Could you please check it?" I heard some muffled words and felt the wires move slightly by my head. Dr. Edgerton shook his head at me. "Your batteries have run out. I only have a little more to do on your chin. Can you hold on for me?"

I started to nod my head and smile, but caught myself in time and murmured, "Mmm hmm," hoping that he would understand. I was trapped and had no choice. He had been his usual kind self, thinking of my feelings, though he wanted to finish, as any artist would.

I tried to imagine I was still listening to the tape. I did not allow myself to slip away into the cold sterile terror of the operating room. My life vest of Hemi-Sync was gone. Would I drown? I felt a goldfish-sized thought form that the pain might be ten times greater without my tape. I visualized my face with closed eyes. I told the pain signals to go away with 55515. I willed myself to remember that I had done this before. I would overcome this latest challenge; I must clutch shreds of calm tightly to my inner self. I amazed myself by faintly savoring that relaxing peace with each careful breath.

As he finished, Dr. Edgerton patted my shoulder. "You were terrific, Gari. Do you have extra batteries? I'll send someone up to your room for them while you are in Recovery if you'd like."

I moved my eyes from left to right and said, "Unh, unh," still not moving my face. Why didn't I think of bringing extra batteries with me? I would *never* do that again. Dr. Edgerton sent someone to buy some in the gift shop, and they were brought to me in the Recovery Room. I understood how a dehydrated, dying man feels when being given a drink of water. I had not panicked, but I was getting anxious for my "tape fix." What a wonderful relief to listen to Robert Monroe's soothing calm voice again and feel balanced by those familiar tones!

Soon, I was wheeled from Recovery back to my room. My face felt tight, puffy, and different. At least now, mirrors were not hidden from me, so I could have a look when I wanted.

Mum was waiting for me in my room. She said, "You were amazing again, Darling. The surgery went well. You have a nice rest now. I put your Magic Slate on the bedside table." I smiled goodbye, switched to the "Pain Control" tape and blissfully slept. I later found out that the surgery had lasted five hours, hence the batteries' death.

When I awakened the next day, I forgot that my face would be changed another time. Unconsciously, I tried to yawn; it did not happen. I felt a tight barrier over the front of my face, as if I were in an iron mask. I knew I was in the hospital again for another surgery but forgot, in that instant of waking, what had happened this time. Would I ever be back in a normal life with a normal face and easy familiarity? I did not realize how much I valued it until it was snatched from me. Slowly, I remembered about the grafting flaps for lips, plus cheek and chin revision, as I felt twinges of pain stir the concrete tightness. I reached over for my trusty tape player and started the "Energy Walk" tape. I liked that side of the tape best. It was important for me to coddle myself in any way possible. Quickly, the pain signals receded with the help of the tape. I knew I could do it on my own, but the back-up of using the tape was reassuring. After the tape ended, I got up with my I.V. pole and shuffled into the bathroom, where I could see my new stage of a face. I was surprised to see two big long incisions running from the top lip area to the base of my nose. Now, in addition to having all the other scars, I looked as if I had a cleft palate. How could the doctors make my appearance worse? All the skin was gathered in the mouth area into a huge burst of lip tissue in the center. It looked like a fish mouth that little kids try to imitate—how ugly! There was a tiny hole on the left side of the mouth with a plastic tube fitted inside, just big enough to insert a Brecht feeder tube. Remembering the feeder tubes, I wanted a drink of water. I realized I would have to rise above my feelings of frustration and get my act together by finding a glass, as well as the Brecht feeder.

The hole did not look large enough to get a toothbrush inside. My tongue felt raw, as did the parts of my mouth I gently touched with it. When I rubbed sutures with my tongue, I was afraid that I might rip them loose, so I resolved to keep my tongue still. My mouth felt dirty and tasted of old blood, making me want to spit up. I realized in terror that there was no way that I could, with the tiny hole the doctors had left me. Just the idea that vomit would have to be swallowed filled me with horror and pity for myself. Inside the mouth, I opened my jaws a tiny bit, but it pulled and stabbed my face. I would have to be careful not to tear open sutures. The cheeks and chin were roadmaps of new incisions and stitches. They looked puffy and tight, with three long incisions from my bottom lip to my chin, across the lower part of my face. There was a big metal loop, about which I was not told beforehand, taped above my lips as a brace. The only positive thought I could manage was that the freak I saw in the mirror was "Me In Transition" instead of "The Real Me" for the future.

I went back to my bed and found, alongside the Magic Slate, a carafe of water, a glass, and, thoughtfully, a new selection of Brecht feeders and tubes. I selected a narrow tube and syringe and took them into the bathroom to rinse the rubber and plastic taste out of them. I was clumsy putting it together, out-of-practice again. I successfully inserted the tiny tube into the even tinier opening in my mouth and savored the lovely cold trickle of water dribbling down my throat. I wondered if I could put water inside my mouth and swish it around and spit it out to clean my mouth, since I could not brush. When I tried, I could not make anything come out the hole. Was this the way the end of drooling would happen? This was not the solution I had envisioned. Every operation seemed to bring new adjustments which I never thought about in advance. If I had been told I would have to deal with a dirty mouth and bad breath for the length of the graft-taking, I might have balked at the procedure. The doctors revealed only the good of each surgery in advance. I resented the unpleasant surprises afterwards; I would have plenty of questions when the doctors arrived.

Mum arrived and was impressed at how good my color was the day after surgery, unlike the other times when I looked like white waxed paper. In my role as cheerful patient, I wrote to her on the Magic Slate, "I'm glad you remembered to bring this for me! I never thought of it." As the residents and interns arrived, I realized with a stab of sadness that I could not smile anymore, as I usually did when they entered the room. Another Major Loss along with vomiting!

Dr. Persing inspected the graft. "We were lucky, Gari. You had enough palate skin left to get good tissue for your new lips. With your cheeks and chin, we pulled skin from the sides of your face, just as we did for your nose. This is why it feels very tight to you. This is the opposite direction from a face lift. Don't ever try to have one later on, as we couldn't leave you enough skin. Your surgery lasted five hours because we had to make two Abbe grafting flaps, instead of one as we planned, to obtain enough vermillion from what was left to use inside your mouth. The next surgery will have to be put off until you've healed for four weeks, not two as you were told, due to the complications. You'll need to eat with the Brecht feeder until the graft has taken. At that time, we can reshape the living tissue into lips. Dr. Edgerton is concerned about your being far away in Colorado during the four weeks of healing, in case of any problems. Is there anywhere you could stay closer to us?"

Mum immediately interjected, "She can go home with me to Philadelphia, which is much closer than Denver."

"That would be fine. Dr. Edgerton knows other doctors there, who could take care of small problems for us with the graft if necessary. If any major problems happen, we would need her back here."

All this was suspiciously smoothly orchestrated. I wondered if it had been arranged in advance between my mother and the doctors. Would I ever be in control of my life again? I realized that I would have an easier time healing in a peaceful house, without all the problems and violence in my own. I had not envisioned being unable to talk for four weeks. I resolved to live through this and survive as I had before. I worried about Tom and the dog and cat without me to protect them from Charlie. I would have to abdicate motherhood for a while. I wrote on my slate, "How can I brush my teeth during this waiting period between surgeries? I have a mouth of new teeth to protect."

Dr. Persing smiled and answered, "I'm afraid you won't be able to get a toothbrush inside your mouth. The best I can tell you is to try to squirt the tube as far back as possible in your throat to keep the mouth clean. After you've eaten, use the Brecht feeder to rinse out with clear water, or salt water if you can stand to swallow it. You won't be able to spit anything out. It's important not to strain the graft area. Keep your face as immobile as possible and don't pull your mouth apart. You may have your I.V. tubes removed, since you've recovered so well. Good Luck!"

I hated the prospect of not being able to brush my new hard-won teeth. I was afraid that they would disintegrate, while my mouth was sewn up for a month. I wondered why lips were not made before teeth. Then I remembered that the building block shape had to be under the skin first. It was just like my rib/nose and grafted cheeks and jaws. Building a face surely was slower than building a house.

The herd of doctors left, and I wrote to Mum, "Thanks for offering to keep me again. Will this fit into your plans?"

"Of course, darling," she said. "I'll call Colorado and tell George. You write on your slate what you want me to say, and I'll do your talking."

I felt guilty not returning to being the needed wife and mother. I wrote, "Please say how sorry I am that I can't come back as planned, especially with the house in such a mess. Find out how everyone is, even Peggy and Molly."

Mum explained that the doctors had refused to let me be far from them while the graft was starting to grow, so I had no choice but to come home with her. George said that everyone was fine and I was not to worry.

Chapter 12

The next day Mum and I drove to Philadelphia after I was released from the hospital. I still felt guilty going to Mum's. It was a relief to know that I did not have to face the problems in Denver while weak and unable to talk. The Monroe tapes helped greatly in achieving calmness and diverting pain. They could not, however, remove my anguish at failing to be a good wife and mother. I had learned earlier how isolated being unable to speak made me feel, and I resented losing what I had just regained. It seemed harder the second time to be away from speech. I could not shout for help. Not only could I not run to escape if I were in a fire; I couldn't even call for anyone to rescue me. I quickly remembered to carry my Magic Slate everywhere I went. It took me hours longer to write than to speak, so I did not bother with most of my thoughts. I kept my communication to the basic necessities and spent most of my time reading or knitting.

It was spring in the real world. Outside my window, the apple trees were bursting with fuzzy new leaves and tiny white blossoms. This year I could smell the newness of the season. But I could not speak to tell anyone the joy I saw or smelled. This beautiful new world was lonely, though surrounded by people. I kept reminding myself that this stage, too, would pass.

Mum tried to get me to go with her on errands. I shied away from the stares which I knew to be out in the real world. I was happier protected at home, immersing myself in books. Due to concern that I might move my face while sleeping, Mum wanted to tape my mouth and face tightly closed at night. I already felt like the *Man in the Iron Mask* and recoiled at the idea of any more facial restraints. I knew she was just trying to help me heal, but no one could understand my terror each time I lost more of my limited freedoms. The second time, it really was harder to keep my hope and optimism intact. I wondered if my life would ever feel perfect and complete again. Mum called Colorado for me several times a week. I would listen to George telling me how terrific things were. Next, Tom would tell me about his school and his new friends. Charlie did not want to talk to me. After listening, I would write questions, which Mum would ask for me, before handing me the receiver again. I realized that deaf people are even more isolated than the blind. I felt that everyone was telling me that everything was fine so that I would not worry and would heal faster. I wondered if I were getting the real truth in these conference calls. Since Dr. Persing had said that there was no way that the second surgery could be done sooner, I just had to wait, practicing patience and hoping for the best.

I discovered several books which helped me during this period. Just when I most needed it, I began reading a wonderful book which a friend had recommended, *You Can Heal Your Life* by Louise L. Hay. It was filled with positive affirmations and encouragement. One of the first instructions was to look into a mirror and repeat out loud, "I love and approve of myself." I found this hard to do, looking at my mangled face without a voice. I forced myself to whisper it silently each time I looked into a mirror. Slowly, the phrase became more natural to think whenever I saw a mirror. I also read *Pathfinders*, by Gail Sheehy, which inspired me to decide how I could use my accident as a beneficial turning point in my life, just as the subjects in the book had done with their individual tragedies. I identified with the descriptions of the balance of life in Africa from Laurens van der

Post's books, *A Story Like the Wind* and *A Far Off Place*, and Madeleine L'Engle's ways of achieving peace in *The Small Rain* and *A Circle of Quiet*. Books certainly were my best friends again.

Meals were a pleasure to smell and observe, with anticipation for my future. Usually, we would all eat in the dining room. I was glad to be able to choose what I wanted, instead of being limited to the hospital bouillon, Jell-o, and soup. I was also grateful to have real food ground up, instead of jars of baby food. Usually I could manage oatmeal and juice for breakfast, with my smelly powdered vitamins mixed in. One morning, while trying to squirt in the disgusting mixture, the tube clogged. Dark brown stickiness exploded all over my face and clothes. My eyes burst into tears and my mouth wanted to cry. I realized that I would have to laboriously clean my face all over again, and I was sure that the gluey oatmeal stains would probably ruin my clothes.

Mum jumped up and said, "It will all come out in the wash. Come on and I will help you clean up. It is not a tragedy, I promise!" How glad I was to have her as my mother!

For lunch, Mum would have a beautifully arranged salad with cottage cheese, yogurt, and fruit, while my stepfather had soup and a sandwich. I savored the smell of his grilled cheese. I wanted one for my very own, the first day I had an open mouth and real lips. I ate soup with my Brecht feeder—a different flavor each day. After lunch, we would nap while I listened to a Monroe tape. Dinner would smell even more tantalizing. I relished the look and aroma of each dish. I was given ground-up leftovers in little bowls, with my collection of Brecht feeders. Mum tried to keep a conversation going, undaunted by the fact that I could not answer without my Magic Slate. She asked only yes-or-no questions so I could nod my head and not have to stop eating to write on the Magic Slate. After dinner I would go to bed and read before going to sleep with a Monroe tape.

It was not a very exciting existence. But resting and healing do happen faster when one's life is peaceful.

My husband flew to Philadelphia to see me midway between surgeries. It felt wonderful to feel his strong arms around me and enjoy a real hug again! He seemed distant, however, without the same tenderness and caring he showed before. I wondered if this was from the stress of caring for Charlie. Had I been looking for another father in this marriage? Was he looking for a bright, cheerful accident victim he could protect, but in whom he had lost interest? I tried to put all those feelings out of my mind. I concentrated on positive thoughts: Tom and Charlie were doing well in their new school, and I savored feeling part of a couple again with the special sharing and planning for the future. When he left, I counted the days until my return.

Finally, after I had read about a thousand books, it was time to return to the University of Virginia Hospital. Mum helped me pack up, trying not to cry. "Just remember that if you ever need me, I can be on a plane right away. It takes just a minute to pick up the telephone. In Colorado, you seem so far away. In Virginia, I always felt I could get in my car and see you."

I wrote, "I KNOW! I LOVE YOU!" We both had tears in our eyes. I did not dare cry and risk losing control and moving my sewn-up jaw. I swallowed lots, trying to smile with my eyes, as we hugged.

The drive to Virginia was lovely, with dogwood trees in bloom and shrubs, flowers, and tiny new grass bursting with spring. I was glad to see my favorite countryside that season. We did not stop at the shop. My appearance would be a problem if customers were around, and I could not talk anyway. I had realized by then that I should put the shop up for sale. It was harder for me to manage at a distance, and I needed to put my energy into healing and trying to make my new marriage work. It was devastating to think of losing my identity of a successful business owner, but perhaps someone who loved it as much would buy it.

We went through our usual routine of my checking into the University Hospital and Mum checking into Howard Johnson's. By then I knew all the nurses on the plastic floor and Mum knew all the hotel personnel, as well as the nurses. I was soon upstairs, greeting everyone with my Magic Slate. Magically, I was given a window bed by a lovely budding magnolia tree.

Dr. Edgerton came by with the residents and interns that evening. He looked carefully at my mouth and said, "What a lovely little rosebud you have grown for us, Gari. It looks healthy and perfect for the work we'll do tomorrow. We plan to separate the graft and make upper and lower lips from it. We'll work a little on your chin and right cheek to give them shape. This surgery should be shorter than the last. Do you plan to use the Monroe tapes again? More importantly, do you have new batteries this time for your tape player?"

I smiled with my eyes as I wrote a giant "YES" on my Magic Slate.

He said, "I'd like to listen to one of your Emergency Series tapes. You're more relaxed using them in the Operating Room. I wondered if my other patients could benefit from them. When this surgery is over, could I please borrow one to try?"

I pointed to my Magic Slate "Yes" and wished I could smile.

Then he asked, "Would you like me to refine your tracheotomy scar on your throat, if we have time?"

I nodded an emphatic yes and pointed to my Magic Slate. I wrote, "The area still stabs back to my spine each time I swallow. Maybe you could look for the reason, when you open up that scar area."

"I'll do my best," he said, patting me on the shoulder.

The evening and morning were easy, with the trusty tapes to rely upon. I felt like such an old hand at operations now. I knew the nurses and doctors and the routine on the floor. I had a nice roommate who had been there before also, which helped me feel more at home. In the morning the orders got mixed somehow and I was given a double dose of Valium before going down to the operating room. Mum laughed with me as I became more and more mellow and "loved the whole world." I used the Monroe "Inter-Op" tape again in the operating room and found it even more effective as I gained practice. The surgery flashed by. I was still incredibly happy after the surgery, in the Recovery Room and back in my own bed, due to my drunkenness from the Valium. I wondered if this was how people who took drugs regularly felt.

When I looked in the mirror, I was relieved to see real lips on my face at last, though sprinkled with sutures. What a magician Dr. Edgerton was! Incredibly, he had made what looked like the beginnings of lips from that fish-face of a graft! Each surgery gave me more respect for the long studies, vision, and practice which go into reconstruction of the human body. My chin was slowly taking shape and beginning to stick out like a real one. My right cheek was less sunken, and, best of all, the tracheotomy scar was a tiny thin line now instead of a big jagged lump. When I swallowed, it no longer grabbed me with pain as if there were a vise around my throat. That made me even more sure that I really did love the world, but especially Dr. Edgerton for taking that pain away.

Mum was relieved that I was sober the next morning. Lee and Blair came to visit and brought beautiful white and purple lilacs as well as orange, red, and green parrot tulips from their respective gardens. Mr. Clark came in to say a prayer for me and exchange news. Dr. Langman dropped by, and it was helpful to be able to ask about dealing with Charlie.

She said, "If a man on the street said 'I hate you' to you, it wouldn't matter so much. You need to let go of your feelings of responsibility for him and keep your communications to a minimum. Let his father deal with him as much as possible. You need to make your own healing your priority."

When Dr. Edgerton came by to check on my progress, he told me that he had removed an adhesion the size of a little finger, which had grown around my vocal cords behind the tracheotomy incision. This had caused the pain when I swallowed and talked. He said that my voice might improve markedly with this growth gone. He also said that I could go home in a few days, but that I must stay on the Brecht feeder for a few weeks and not brush my teeth yet, as the lips needed to heal without anything disturbing them. A former resident of his, now in private practice in Denver, could take out the sutures in two weeks. I would need to return in September, for more work on the chin. Dr. Chuong told me to chew and bite on the side of my mouth after the lips healed. It would help while the lips were tender to try to keep my lips from touching forks, spoons or my toothbrush.

I grinned and said, "Thank you all so much for this next stage of my face. The best is swallowing freely again and having real lips. Someday I'll learn to kiss again."

That night, my roommate and I went to a pizza party down the hall. I felt as if I were in a college dorm. Everyone else had pizza, while I had my Brecht-feeder meal. I was satisfied by smelling the wonderful crispy, spicy, tomato aroma. I knew my time would come again. The party was in Debbie Fox's room. She was the girl born without a face or hand, whose book I had read years ago. Dr. Edgerton had worked on her at Johns Hopkins Hospital, moving her eyes from the sides to the front of her face. She looked terrifically normal to me, from my stage of reconstruction. She told me she was in for minor corrections this time. I was amazed watching her use her agile hand with fingers made from her toes. Again, I thought how lucky we all were to have Dr. Edgerton shape our lives.

The next day, I thanked all the nurses and doctors

and then Mum drove me to Washington to fly back to Denver, giving me last-minute advice on dealing with my life. We had a lovely lunch with clam chowder and ice cream through my Brecht feeder for me and a salad for her, before we said goodbye. She had nurtured me overwhelmingly in my new life. I would miss her being nearby. In my optimistic way, I felt excited to return to love and happiness with my husband, ignoring the ugly memories of Charlie.

George met me at the airport with a giant, careful hug. He told me how beautiful my new lips were and what fun it would be, when they healed, to try them out. The dog and cat and boys ran to the door to welcome me as we arrived home. Tom gave me a bear hug and said "Grr." Charlie even joined in the family welcome. The mountains were crisp and stark behind the softness of my forsythia bush's yellow mass of blooms. We went out to dinner—which was soup and a milkshake for me—and I bubbled over with happiness to be part of a family again. How could I not heal quickly, surrounded by such love and caring?

Chapter 13

The day after my arrival, I did mundane things—unpacked five boxes, did four loads of laundry and three loads of dishes, in addition to weeding the garden and cleaning the pool. Of course, trying to be Wonder Woman again, I was exhausted. I lost patience with Charlie when he terrorized three little children in the neighborhood. When the mothers called me to complain, I apologized and felt mortified.

We went to a neighborhood party later that evening where I met the callers. Everyone was very friendly and understanding. I drank some wine with my Brecht feeder and felt lucky to be with congenial people. The wives who lived nearby told me to call them anytime I needed anything. They had all moved from somewhere else and knew how lonely one could feel.

In two weeks, I went to Dr. Edgerton's former resident, Dr. Richard Albin, to have the stitches out of my lips, chin, and throat. I felt it was a picnic compared to former painful memories. I was not sure whether I was getting tougher or the doctors were gentler. He said to continue for about ten more days with the Brecht feeder and then I could begin eating and brushing my teeth after my return to have the pull lines out of my throat and chin. Pull lines are long single sutures stitching skin together like a seam, attached only at each end. They are used for straight scars to help them heal closer and neater. To remove them, the doctor clips the two ends and quickly pulls out the line under the skin.

The ten days passed in a flash. I awakened filled with excitement on the day I was to have the final suture pull lines out, until I looked outside. The lovely blooming landscape was covered in snow, falling hard and fast. How could this happen on the day I had to drive alone all the way downtown? I dressed warmly and started out ahead of time. I was determined not to be afraid in the snow and to avoid other drivers like the plague. I soon discovered the magic of Denver snow: the climate is dry, so snow melts very quickly on roads, lingering only on grass and trees, and road signs. I was glad I knew where I was going, because all the street signs were white. I arrived safely, taking tiny careful steps on the slippery sidewalk into the office, so as not to fall and hurt my carefully reconstructed face.

I was afraid to have the pull lines out, remembering the pain from the graft on my abdomen when it was pulled, but this time the lines were shorter and the hand swifter. I let out my tensely held breath in relief. Now I could forget being a patient for a few months and be free. I was thrilled to hear Dr. Albin tell me that I could put away the Brecht feeders again.

The driving was not as bad going home as I feared, though the snow was getting deeper. I was relieved to drive into the garage and be home to stay. But then I heard strange noises in the house and found the dog and cat shivering with fear as the boys fought. They had been sent home from their schools due to the projected blizzard. Charlie, who had been transferred to another school for special education while I had been away, was like a bomb ready to explode, keeping the rest of us always on edge. I stopped the fight and wondered how I could ever heal in this atmosphere.

At dinner that night, I proudly set my place with a real knife, fork, and spoon. What a difference from my Brecht feeder collection! I cooked a delicious meal of chicken, asparagus, and rice to eat with my real lips. With the first bite, however, I encountered disaster. My fork hit my cheek instead of my mouth, and all the chicken fell on my plate. Charlie laughed, pointing at me; the others ignored him. My new mouth was narrower and not in the same spot. I put a smaller bite on the fork and carefully lined it up, successfully getting it inside. I realized that I would have to take very small, ladylike bites forever. The size of the lips, as well as what I could manage to fit inside the narrow palate, had to be my guide. I smiled to myself with pride that I could eat a real bite again, although I knew I would need to practice in front of a mirror. As I looked around the table, Charlie yelled, "This tastes like dog food. I'm not eating it!" He ran away from the table. I remembered "The Pig" and let George handle him. I tried to begin a conversation with Tom about his soccer team.

A slim ray of hope opened for me when I noticed a hatha yoga class being taught at the local recreation center. I missed the discipline of exercise and wondered if I could participate despite my limitations and deformities. From the first class, the teacher, Kathy, was a steady inspiration in my life, just as my original teacher, Yusuf, had been. She noticed me struggling to move my legs into positions and said, "Gari, don't worry about what you can or can't do yet. Your body has the memory of what you have done before and eventually it will all come back to you." I was to remember what she said whenever I became discouraged in the future. I found my favorite part of class was the final relaxation time, as my rusty muscles re-learned to stretch.

School was soon over. Tom left for camp and Charlie for his mother's. George and I, for the first time in our brief marriage, were to have a whole month alone without children. He was not the same as before, however. I felt our relationship had changed, and I wondered if we each had fallen in love with an illusion. Had we traded one set of problems for another? Getting to know George was like peeling an onion. I felt he had many of the same characteristics as his son, a thought which terrified me. I was sure that he was equally disillusioned about me, though I hoped we could sort things out this month. I wondered if our major differences could be merged.

I made an appointment with George's dentist and went in to have my teeth cleaned like a Real Person. The technician was careful touching my sensitive grafted lips and new mouth, but I was not the ideal patient. I had sensations in strange places in my mouth, due to all the tissue and nerves being relocated. I longed for it to be over, so I could go home and forget being hurt. My gums bled and smarted; I drooled uncontrollably down my chin. The dentist said that I would have to be vigilant about keeping my mouth clean and showed me how to floss under my bridges. He ripped floss and pain under the teeth. I did not think I could ever do that torture to myself. He said to begin with a toothpick, scraping around my gums, then floss, then brush and finish up with a Waterpik rinse. It was going to take me hours to clean my mouth now, and would hurt in the process. I knew I did not have enough bone in my jaw left to ever manage dentures, so I had to do what I was told. How I wished I could go back in time and change the course of my life!

George and I found that our month alone passed too quickly. We regained some of our original closeness without the disruptions, but we needed more time. All six children arrived on the fourth of July, full of enthusiasm for their Colorado summer vacation. We invited friends over to watch fireworks, and George got sparklers for the children. As we were beginning to cook hamburgers on the grill, Charlie set off a loud firecracker right by my elderly dog Peggy, knowing that she was terrified by noises. I was furious at his thoughtlessness but let George discipline him as I tried to soothe the terrified dog. I tried to forget Charlie's meanness and be a good hostess, but I realized that one certainly does judge stepchildren by behavior.

The next day, I left the girls and Charlie at home alone while I picked up some milk for their lunch.

I returned to a disaster. In twenty minutes, Charlie had kicked, hit, and terrorized the others, flooded two floors of the house, and locked himself in his bedroom, screaming that he was going to commit suicide with his penknife. My daughter called George for help. We arrived together. George dealt with Charlie, and I bandaged cuts, calmed the weeping girls, mopped up water, and carried flooded boxes and furniture from the cellar outside to dry. I began to think that maybe this was not going to work out.

After George was home that night and I was off guard duty, I took a long walk with the dog on the greenbelt, to think alone. There was a lovely peaceful pink, pale blue, and white sky, which returned my inner balance. Peggy kept stopping to investigate the giant big puffs of dandelions and tall cattails in the stream, where a quiet mallard family watched her cautiously. How could I have gotten myself into such a violent, stressful situation in the middle of such peace and beauty? Later, when I talked to Mum about the disaster, I asked if she thought that I had rebounded into an easy solution for the previous problems. She reminded me again of the pig getting up and slowly walking away. I resolved to myself to keep on trying.

The next day, as I watched Emily put on lipstick, I said sadly, "I wish I could still do that."

"Your lips have healed enough now, Mummy. Let me teach you this time," she said as she gave me her lipstick. We laughed as I clumsily covered my upper lip with red. "Now you blot your two lips together like this." I tried but could not make my new face and lips do it. I remembered doing that tiny movement automatically with my first face. My new muscles would not listen and obey me.

"Maybe you need to outline your lips," she said as she tried to do it for me. The edges were all rumply and looked like a clown; but Emily has never been known for giving up easily. She wiped me off for several more tries in vain. My lips were sore when she decided, "You must need to heal more, but you can practice smushing your lips together so you will be ready."

I tried over the years without success. All color smeared and blurred within minutes. Furthermore, I could not do without the protection of sunscreen on my lips, just to step outside; the grafted lip skin burned from hot spicy foods or sun. I had to remember that I was a Bionic Woman in my Second Life.

Suddenly, my shop sold. I had to fly back and close out everything with the help of Mary and Louise. Though it was a sad ending, I was happy to know that it was bought by a person who loved it as much as I did and that both Mary and Louise were to continue to work for the new owner. I felt as if I were letting go of a child who had grown up.

I drove up the coast after the closing, collecting advice about my problems. I visited a friend in Washington, who asked if I had a glimmer of caring left in my marriage. If not, I should break it off now and not linger with the violence and anger before it increased; if I did still care, I should return and try harder to overcome the problems with counseling. My stepmother's advice was to get out while I could because Charlie was going to be that way a long time. Mum and my stepfather felt that only I could decide what to do, but they wanted me to think about whether I felt I had really given the situation a chance.

We all cried as I left for Denver. I realized how much I depended upon them in my fledgling second life. They supported me flinging myself out on my tiny new wings, even when nothing seemed to be there except empty air. Would I ever sing with joy like a bird again?.

The house was full of tension, anger, and negativity upon my return. I arranged for Charlie's counselor to meet with the whole family to discuss each individual's feelings. The children were asked to say what they liked and did not like about each other, a process which gave us all a new perspective. Then the counselor told the children they could leave the room and asked George and me how we felt. George began by discussing divorce. I realized that our marriage was over. George and I discussed how we would sever our six-month-long marriage. The logistics proved to be simple, since there were hardly any things to divide. We shared the attorney expenses and went out to lunch together afterwards. We both felt a great sense of relief, though we were sad that our original dream had not worked out.

When I called Mum, she was wonderfully consoling and reminded me that she would always be there for me. My children were supportive and told me of other dreadful things which had happened in Denver in their private childworld. I felt glad that I had ended the bad situation. I was relieved that I would no longer have to be a policewoman but sad to let my dream of a happy marriage end.

Alone without a man in my life again, I found little things, such as a trip to the market or the mall, of paramount importance to plan. I noticed couples everywhere and felt afraid to go places alone. My left hand felt empty without my wedding ring. I needed to learn to do without the status or dependency of marriage. I realized that a marriage can be wrong, ending from a joint failure, not an individual one. The people involved still have fine qualities. I had many good things in my life for which to be thankful—terrific children, comfortable house and pool, inspiring view of the Rockies, loving cat and dog, supportive family and friends, and thoughtful neighbors. Tom and I spent time talking and healing together. We began taking little trips with picnics to discover the surrounding mountains and old mining towns. We drove up Mount Evans, the Mecca for traditional tours of quaking aspen trees, as they changed from summer green to shimmery gold each fall.

My hard contact lenses had been uncomfortable and blurry since I had moved to a dry climate, but

Dr. Edgerton preferred that I not have the weight of glasses on the new nose. I went to an optometrist who introduced me to oxygen-permeable lenses. He felt they would help my eyes retain the tears while letting oxygen into the corneas. They made a very comfortable change to my life. Suddenly, I had a new, clearer world to see.

One of the first visions was my son's spur-of-the-moment Mohawk haircut. Tom and some neighborhood boys spent an inordinate amount of time in his bathroom one day; he emerged with a tiny strip of hair along the top of his head. He liked it for about a half-hour and then wanted his hair back. Unfortunately, it was just like my first face and did not magically reappear. He went to school the next day with his ski jacket hood firmly tied in place under his chin. He returned home to say he was the talk of the school and his class loved it. However, we had to find him a hat with flaps in the back to hide his neck that afternoon. The next day, he learned to turn the laughter around so that he was laughing together with the group. My lack of confidence was in my missing face and his was in his missing hair. We empathized with each other.

Chapter 14

When the University of Virginia called with my next surgery date, I felt the old pocket of fear begin to grow in the solar plexus. I wanted to cry and have a strong man to hold and take care of me. I did not want to be grown up and brave and strong all the time. I wondered if I could manage a surgery all by myself, and I felt apprehensive of the change to come from the next reconstruction. What would I look like next? Mum would not be able to be with me beforehand at the hospital; I felt bereft of my main support from before. As Tom often reminded me, I was a Big Girl and had to act like one, though I did not always want to do so.

Despite my worries, everything soon fell into place. Tom's father offered to keep him while I was in the hospital. Kindly, he also volunteered to pick us up at the airport and deliver me to the University of Virginia. Emily was away at boarding school, but would come home for the weekend and visit me in the hospital. Since she and Tom were to spend this Christmas with their father, I looked forward to the chance to see her. My funny cousin Annie called to say that I could not have all the glory of being the only one in the family getting a second divorce. She was going through one also. She suggested spending Christmas together in Mexico to have fun. I jumped at the chance to have a trip to look forward to, making my surgical near-future not as bleak.

Arriving at the University of Virginia Hospital now was similar to going to see good friends. I knew the people in Admitting as well as the nurses and doctors on the Plastic Surgery floor and remembered to ask about details of their lives that we had discussed during my last stay. I was gifted with a window bed again, facing another direction with a new view. I think that some kind soul must have put *WINDOW* in capital letters on my patient record. Whoever admitted me always said "You prefer a window, don't you?" as if they were asking about an airline seat.

The contingent of doctors, headed by Dr. Persing, came by in the evening to discuss what would be done the next day. The lips would be sculpted more, the chin reshaped, and my longest knee scar from the engine reduced. This meant that I would have to keep my right leg straight for six months; but it would be worth it to lose that huge, ugly raised lump which snaked around my knee. I longed for all my scars to blend into me, ceasing to be the first thing people noticed about me. I reminded the doctors that I would be using my Monroe Tapes in the operating room and for pain control afterwards. They accepted them as a fact of life for me by now.

That night when all was quietish and dark, I lay in bed overwhelmed by anguish and loneliness. I missed having the security and reassurance of my mother. Would I be strong enough to survive yet another surgery the next day? I understood how soldiers felt the night before battle. I longed for someone to give me a compassionate hug to erase my forlornness. My soul was exhausted, keeping a smile for the public while I wept silently inside. Tears of self-pity streaked down my cheeks. I stared, without seeing, at the ugly green hospital chair and trite painting of a field and pond on the wall above it. As I wallowed in despair, the room slowly changed. The chair gave off a glowing aura, as did the painting, the bedside table, the foot of the bed, and even the silent television impaled high on the wall. They exuded a lovely happiness which embraced me, like a shiny Christmas tree. Suddenly I *understood*, with a flash of peace in my heart. All these ugly things were there to help me heal, just like doctors and nurses. I realized that I should never feel alone again; we are constantly surrounded by love and healing wherever we are. The green chair was teaching me just what I tried to teach others about myself: inside an ugly exterior beams a true shining light. In my first life, I concentrated on the exterior lampshades, instead of the inner lights. The whole sweep of my journey to find myself was resolved in that instant. I whispered "Thank you" to the glowing green chair and the radiating room. I turned on my tape player to ready myself for the battle of surgery the next day.

I awoke with the comforting memory of the vision the night before. I smiled at my chair, without fear of what was to come. The morning went smoothly, using the stepping stones of the tapes. I felt calm and happy and knew that I was in the best hands.

The surgery lasted five hours instead of the hour planned. Once Dr. Edgerton began, his love of precision always made him find more to correct; he was an artist who needed to put one more brush stroke on the canvas. He grafted a tiny bit more onto my top lip from my palate, to fill it out and even up the two lips, made Z-shapes out of the straight lines on my chin scars so they would blend into the face, sculpted an indentation below my lips to separate them from the chin, and neatened up the knee scars. I forgot pain using the tapes.

Mum arrived, relieved that I was all right. Yusuf, my yoga teacher, came by to tell me he was selling his health food store and going to medical school. His first hospital visit after my accident started him thinking about becoming a doctor. I was happy to hear his news because he would be a gift of a wonderful, caring doctor for the world. Lee and Blair thoughtfully brought cheerful flowers again, as Emily, Tom, and their father arrived. Emily was less and less disturbed by my appearance by now, and she was able to rub oil on my forehead where it was dry from the surgical scrubbing. Dr. Edgerton popped in while all the visitors were there and told me not to talk so much and hurt the new lip graft he had worked on that day. My visitors would have to do the talking for me. Everyone laughed and remarked what a thoughtful gentleman he was.

Time passed swiftly during this hospitalization. The small lip graft was not nearly as sore as the large one had been the time before. I was, however, reduced to Brecht feeders again to protect the new vermillion. The chin started to settle in, with its careful daily cleaning. The knee bothered me the most, as it retained swelling. I would keep forgetting not to bend it, though it was tightly bandaged and I was back on crutches. Each of these reconstructive surgeries had felt like one step forward and three steps back into past limitations. But at last I felt that some progress was being made. As Mum had to leave earlier, Tom's father drove us to the airport and found me a wheelchair so that I would not have to walk the long distance to the gate. Flights were delayed due to snow in Denver, but ours finally boarded and took off.

We arrived in another blizzard. I was grateful to the kind neighbors who picked us up at the airport. I never could have managed maneuvering in the snow on crutches alone while Tom carried our bags. We safely got to the house with their help, despite the four-foot-high drifts of snow. When we opened the door, the dog and cat were thrilled to see us, but we heard a strange sound of water rushing. I wondered if the child who had been caring for the animals had left a faucet running. Tom and the neighbors looked in the bathrooms and kitchen and found nothing. Then they checked the cellar and saw that the sprinkler system had burst. They turned off the outside water and stopped the leak. At least I had until spring to have it fixed. I needed to put my feet up and rest. Just as I got settled and was working on unclenching my jaws, the phone rang. Mum was frantic that we had been in a plane or car crash due to the snow. We reassured her, though I felt as if I were the one who needed calming. I needed to heal and rest, not find new traumas to deal with all by myself.

The next day, Tom and I got into the car after he had shoveled the driveway. I could drive with my left foot, keeping the right leg stiffly over the passenger's side. That meant that I could be freer. We drove slowly, in jerky left-footed starts and stops, to the market. I was profoundly grateful to still have a handicapped license plate so we could park close to the door. Tom pushed the cart and carried groceries for me, as I hobbled along. I was a mixture of emotions. I felt triumphant to deliver the needed food home and grateful that, again, thanks to Tom's help, I could overcome the odds against me. But my life seemed to take years longer to accomplish on crutches. My arms ached and I felt captive again. I had to do stairs one-legged, could not bend to sit down, and could not stoop to make beds. All my bending was at the waist. It would be good training for yoga, which I would miss for the six months of keeping that leg immobile. It seemed ironic that the major surgery had been done on my face, but that the knee hurt most. It seemed to stay puffy and swollen and achy forever, requiring more work with tapes.

In two weeks, I was able to have the chin and lip stitches removed. The lower part of my face finally looked and felt better. I was concerned to have such a large area which felt full of Novocaine in my collage of a face. I was told that nerves do regenerate themselves sometimes and that time would tell (again). I was to continue with the Brecht feeders for two more weeks, until I returned to have the knee pull lines taken out. If the lip graft had healed enough by that time, then I could go back to a grownup fork and knife.

During this period, all my emotions erupted to the surface of my being. I grew tired quickly and wept at tiny things which normally would have amused me. I was terrified of falling, and I did not think I could get up alone without bending my knee. Tom was wonderfully patient and supportive when I walked on my crutches in the snow. Our roles certainly had been reversed drastically. Now, he reminded me that I was a Big Girl and could do anything I tried. It was a good insight for me of what a wonderful parent he would be in the future. When he was at school, I stayed home and wrote in my journal or read, with my leg propped up to heal. I thought a great deal about my last marriage and its problems. We had all tried to help each other in that marriage, but it was not a good mix. I had to remember how terrific it all was while the magic lasted.

In two weeks, I was able to have the pull lines taken out of my knee. I felt a rush of relief to be just me, without any stitches holding my body together. Suddenly, I felt free and amazingly painless again. I wanted to cry with happiness, just from the simple feeling that almost nothing was wrong with me. I was cautioned not to bend the knee, as scars there tended to stretch more than any other part of the body. I was also to keep an Ace bandage for support on the knee all the time and use a crutch for support to walk. This would remind me not to bend it, as well as help in controlling the swelling.

Making an effort to stay inside and keep warm, I slowly healed with my leg straight. I now appreciated the ease of bending knees to do everyday things, since I had lost that ability. I missed the use of my knee and did not feel that I would ever take it for granted again. After Tom left for Christmas with his father, I had a few days alone, but I managed until I was to leave to join my cousin Annie for our house party in Puerta Vallarta. I had never been to Mexico and was excited to see it and practice my Spanish.

I flew to San Antonio to meet Annie. I had warned her on the phone that she would probably not recognize me due to my changed face. She assured me that she would. At the time, I never thought how many other people she might see getting off my flight with a crutch and a carved-up face. We knew each other immediately and hugged when I hobbled off the plane. We picked up our wonderful close friendship again as we both talked nonstop. We spent that night at her house and left the next day for Mexico.

Annie was nervous about flying, and we were late at the airport, filling out immigration forms in a flurry. When we landed in Mexico City to go through customs, Annie discovered that she had forgotten her passport, but she assured me that she had gotten into the country for years with just her driver's license and Visa card. I showed my passport to the customs agent and was waved through. My cousin began explaining in Spanish that she was accompanying her injured relative to Puerta Vallarta and had only her driver's license and Visa card with her. The agent became suspicious of her excellent Texas Spanish and refused to admit her to the country. We both promptly burst into tears. The rest of the guests were awaiting us in Puerta Vallarta that night. So Annie decided that I should continue on our flight, with my one piece of luggage and her five pieces, find an attorney friend of hers waiting for us in the Puerta Vallarta airport, and send him back to help her get the necessary documents to enter Mexico. She was taken away into detention. I was terrified to be alone in a strange country, not knowing where I was going. I wanted to stay with her and not feel vulnerable, but I realized that her idea was the only sensible one, so set off with my crutch to the next plane.

When the short flight arrived in Puerta Vallarta, I hobbled around on my crutch on the slippery marble floor, looking around for someone who looked like Tom Selleck, from the description Annie had given me, and saw only Mexicans. I had him paged, but the announcement was in such a thick Spanish accent that no American could have recognized his name from it. On my fifth laborious trudge through the airport, I found him at a luggage carousel, and we raced to get him on a flight. When his flight arrived in Mexico City, the customs agents drove Annie out on the tarmac to the plane. They refused to allow any passengers off until she entered and identified him. In wonderfully romantic Mexican fashion, the agents applauded as they emerged. Annie and her friend were then given a temporary pass to go to the American Embassy, where they obtained a visa for the allotted days and finally rejoined the group.

Meanwhile, with the help of a porter, I managed to collect my bag, Annie's assortment of luggage, and a taxi. Annie had told me only the name of the art gallery belonging to the owner of the villa we had rented. It was late, everything was closed, and no one around knew where she lived. My heart sank, as I was tired and I hurt. I also had a mountain of luggage in a strange town, with no place to stay. Luckily my Spanish was adequate; no one seemed to speak English. This was not the way to rest up from surgery in peace and quiet!

I asked the driver to take me to a hotel. He said that he thought all the hotels were filled due to the Christmas season. We tried several, and each time I was told there was no room. Was I to spend the night in a Mexican stable *a la* Mary and Joseph? How would I keep my scars clean? Finally, after the fifth rejection, the driver took pity on me and said that he might know of a hotel with an available free room. At that point, I would have taken anything. The place where he took me looked rather sleazy, but they did have a room. I was so tired and so grateful for a bed that it did not register with me the probable meaning of the sign behind the desk stating rates by the hour, half-day, and night. I thanked the driver, tipping him generously for all his time and trouble. The porter took my compendium of luggage upstairs, as I slowly followed with my crutch. I noticed strange noises for a hotel, and men in the hallways gave me searching looks as we passed. But in my exhaustion I thought they were just the usual stares at a disfigured person with a crutch. I locked the door, barricading Annie's suitcases against it, and collapsed in bed. The next day, I would attempt to find the villa. All I wanted was to sleep, after such a long, stressful day. I wondered about Annie and hoped she was all right but was too tired to stay awake and worry.

The next morning, when I called the gallery to explain who I was and ask how I could get to the villa, the owner said that Annie had called to tell them what had happened. No one knew where I was and they had worried all night. When I told her where I spent the night, she began to laugh. It was a hotel mainly used for assignations. What a way to begin my introduction to Mexico!

Annie's son arrived to collect me and the mountain of luggage. He and a friend had driven a car down, worried that I might fall walking with crutches on the cobblestone streets. I was to be chauffeured through the town in "Christine." Now my Christmas vacation could begin in style.

The villa was inside several extraordinary layers of houses above the coast, all warmly and humidly open to the ocean across the front. Lovely large tile floors glowed under leather and wood Equipali chairs and couches which hugged you inside their softness. Looking down the cliff, I could sit for hours immersed in the changing colors of the ocean. I had never stayed anywhere without windows or screens between me and nature. I adored the openness and lushness of the vegetation. Annie's friends made an unusual house party. I was not used to a life of fun, with people making jokes all the time, and it was a welcome change. My life of worry and incessant work at recovery transformed itself into one where the only concerns were what one would wear to which party each night. We explored the town and countryside; all eight of us piled in the convertible and had giddy fun. We tried a different restaurant for dinner each night before the parties began. I had forgotten how I enjoyed music and dancing, though now I could only watch and dream. It was lovely to laugh again and totally forget my world of surgery and healing at home.

One day, everyone decided to teach me how to put makeup on my new face. I had not used any, due to keeping meticulously clean to heal all the time, except for my disastrous lipstick lesson with Emily. I was thrilled to have many opinions on how to emphasize my remaining good features. The consensus was to draw attention to my best feature and heavily make up my eyes. Mexican eye shadow and liner were borrowed from someone, and each eye was made up differently. Everyone gave an opinion before I was allowed to see myself. I was thrilled to see what a difference a little makeup could do. One guy gave me long lessons in puckering my lips. But it was like Emily's lipstick lesson—I could no longer make kissing noises without feeling in newly grafted skin, and I realized I would have to practice in front of a mirror at home. This new face was slowly becoming acceptable to my new life.

Christmas Eve, as we were on our way to dinner, we came upon a sweet procession of the local children winding around the town square. They were all dressed up in their best clothes, following a costumed Joseph and Mary on a donkey and singing about looking for a place to spend the night as they knocked at the doors of the houses around the square and were turned away. It was charmingly different from the only Christmases I had known, with snow and decorated pine trees. Here the shorter palms outside had twinkly lights, while tiny potted fig trees inside were hung with ornaments. I relished being warm and happy in a foreign land with friends and not having to worry about being strong and brave.

Too soon, the vacation was over, and I returned to Denver and reality. I felt stronger and more able to lead a real life after the trip. Tom had had a wonderful time in Virginia but was glad to return to school and his friends. I realized that I needed to fill my life and not depend upon my son. The next surgery was not to be for at least a year because the major bone building for facial structure was accomplished and needed time for the features to settle into my face. It seemed appropriate to think about employment, so I began sending out my resumé to find a job. I went on several interviews but felt my appearance was a drawback. Also, after having my own business, I was not sure how it would be to work for someone else. Mum, in her weekly call, suggested doing temporary work. I could try out jobs and companies to see what I liked.

I signed up with several temporary agencies. I decided that I really wanted to work for an airline, which had been my dream after college. My parents had felt it was not the best use of my languages, so instead I worked for the Embassy of Bolivia and then the French Embassy in Washington. Both were fascinating jobs, but I never lost the dream of a career with an airline. I did not feel I could return to teaching, as my voice was not strong enough for a class to hear without a microphone. The best way to get my toe in the door was a secretarial job with an airline, and I was thrilled to be called to go to the airport to fill a temporary job in Customer Service with Frontier Airlines.

Dressed in my conservative navy suit, I left very early the first day, not sure how to find my way in the airport to the Customer Service office on Concourse D. I was glad that I could walk without crutches, though I still had to keep my knee as straight as possible. I walked past the office door two times, before I noticed how cleverly it was disguised into the wall. When I entered, the managers welcomed me and showed me my desk and the work piled up waiting for me. It was everything I had hoped—I was in the middle of the action but shielded from public view. If someone could not speak English at a gate and was upset, I would go and calm them down and explain whatever they needed to know. The initial looks of relief, as they heard my first words in their own language, were constant rewards and made me forget the impediment of my face. The people were fun to work with — always joking around, despite working hard on deadlines. By pursuing my dream, I had completed another circle in my life.

I bid on a permanent job with Frontier Airlines and was awarded it, receiving flight benefits and insurance. An airline is like the Army, in that one moves around from department to department and slowly learns all the aspects of running the microcosm. I found each section fascinating in the way in which it fit in with the other goals of keeping planes in shape and flights on time. Employees treat each other like members of a secret society, hidden within the flood of passengers. I felt reassured belonging somewhere again despite the way I looked.

Tom and I took classes in the evenings — Tom learned bike repair, and I took classes on gardening, art, and networking. The networking class had good ideas for making friends in a strange place, which I put to use. I also began attending a support group for divorced people, where I met other singles with the same interests. Eventually, I ended up teaching a class, "How to be Single after Divorce." I began volunteering at the Denver Art Museum, scheduling volunteers for the weekly jazz concerts. These were fun cocktail parties, with local bands playing while people wandered admiring the art collection. I returned to hatha yoga class, while Tom played on football and soccer teams. Our lives grew interesting and settled.

Later in the year, the University of Virginia called to say that I could have a cancellation date in a few months for the next stage of my face. I accepted, but I had major doubts about managing my job as well as healing. I had not accumulated much vacation time, so I would have to take time off without pay. At least I could fly back and forth on a pass, saving money. I told my boss, who was understanding about my situation. I arranged to have someone else cover my job, to give me time to fly to visit Mum briefly, have the surgery, spend a few days in the hospital, and rest a day at home before returning to work. Tom was to visit his father. The neighbors would take care of the dog and cat again. I could let go of my worries and get on with my face.

Chapter 15

Tom and I took off with great excitement for Virginia. I was glad to have the last surgery finally in progress, and Tom looked forward to a week away from school. Mum and my stepfather met us at the airport. We had a hectic visit, talking nonstop. I was glad we could squeeze in this time together; since Mum could not be with me in Charlottesville, she would have worried even more if she had not seen us first. We had an easy flight to Virginia, where Tom's father picked us up and dropped me off at the hospital. It was comforting to see the nurses on the Plastic Surgery floor again. I was no longer surprised to be assigned a window bed. There was no one else in the room; I felt lucky to have the privacy to listen to my Emergency Series tapes. I made my usual sign to tape above the bed—DO NOT TOUCH OR TALK TO PATIENT WHEN PAIN CONTROL TAPES IN USE. I hoped that it would work as well as it had in the past. I still had doubts that I would be strong enough to let something so simple transform my fear and pain into pleasure. I smiled at the standard "ugly" green hospital chair, remembering its lesson for me before the last surgery. I knew now never to doubt that I was protected and loved, despite the momentary feelings of missing both a loving husband in my life and the presence of my fierce mother.

Dr. Edgerton came by with his collection of residents, interns, and students. "How are you, Gari?" he said. "I see that smile is just as pretty."

"Fine, how are you?"

After introducing me to the accompanying men,

he continued, "Tomorrow we will make some more Z's in the straight lines on your chin, to help them recede into the skin. And I need to sculpt the indentation below your lips a little to give you a better profile. Your lips are not quite meeting on one side. We'll adjust a little vermillion, or lip tissue, to even it out. Is there anything that you've noticed which needs work?" I mentioned an enlarged growth on the side of my foot and cysts on the suture lines in my eyelids. Dr. Edgerton said, "Those cysts should come out, before they become any larger. We'll be doing a partial bletheroplasty anyway. We can do a full one, so your upper eyelids will never sag, if you'd like. The foot growth should be removed now, before your shoes are any more uncomfortable. By the way, I enjoyed listening to your Emergency Series tapes. The majority of my patients are concerned with superficial cosmetic appearance, however, and I don't know if they'd be disciplined enough to work with the tapes to use them as successfully as you have. It would be wonderful for them and me if they did. Are you planning to use them again? Did you bring new batteries for your tape player?"

I laughed. "Yes, I will *never* again appear without new batteries. I do want to use the tapes in the Operating Room again, please. What exactly is involved in a bletheroplasty?"

Dr. Edgerton explained, "The name comes from *blepharon,* which means *eyelid* in Greek. An incision, which will later be hidden by the fold in the upper eyelid, is made around the lid. All loose fat, muscle, and skin is removed. At this time, we will also remove the two cysts, which are sticking out on those lids. Because the blood supply is weak to the lids, you will have to be careful for six months not to have your head below your heart. If you do, the lids will swell uncomfortably as they fill with blood. For aftercare with the rest of your face, you will need to eat with the Brecht feeders until the new lip graft has healed, but that's all. How does that sound to you?"

"Fine," I said as the entourage swept out.

Blair and Lee and other friends came to visit that evening. I cherished my long-time friends — it takes interminable effort to find and make new close ones. I went to sleep with dependable Robert Monroe telling me how serene and secure I was. That peaceful feeling was retained in the morning; the confusion of getting ready for the operating room washed over me without disturbing my valuable inner calm. I was grateful once more to The Monroe Institute for giving me control of my life, which I needed.

I was surprised when the orderly wheeled me into the Craniofacial Clinic instead of the operating suite. The head nurse there told me that Dr. Edgerton wanted some more photographs before the surgery. Also, I was to be presented to the whole staff in the auditorium, for discussion about my case, before I went down for surgery. The tapes helped control my agitation at this sudden change. I was glad to know what to expect next. If I planned that I would remain serene for each step — "Pre-Op" preparation, riding in the stretcher, waiting in the cubicle, getting I.V.'s inserted, moving onto the operating table, and the surgery — I needed it all to happen just as I visualized it. Any change might disrupt my fragile balance of serenity and let fear leap inside my unsubstantial protective shell. I clutched my tape player like a precious talisman. I *never* could have survived extra tension like this morning's unexpected changes without my trusty tapes. I kept the "Pre-Op" tape going during the photo session and while sitting alone in the soothing waiting room. Dr. Edgerton's Nurse-Coordinator came in to tell me of a visit she had had from a terrific English lady who had written a book entitled *AboutFace*, about losing her face to cancer, and then began a world organization devoted to helping those with facial deformities. She said that she remembered how alone I had felt going through my reconstruction and offered to lend me her copy of the book to read at home. What a thrill for me to have that to look forward to after this surgery!

Soon, the nurse returned and collected me for the presentation. We walked into a bright, large room, with a small stage at my left and rows of doctors in white coats seated on the right. I did not have my glasses or contact lenses and was afraid of stumbling in my hazy world. The nurse held onto my arm and led me to a chair facing the audience. Dr. Edgerton emerged from the blurry background.

"Good Morning, Gari. You look all ready for our work this morning."

"Good Morning, Dr. Edgerton" was all I had a chance to say before he began lecturing. He described the injuries from my accident and what had been done in each surgery to correct the deformities. I could nearsightedly pick out familiar body shapes with friendly faces in the crowd, as they smiled at me. It was comforting to be the object of this talented group's concern that morning. As Dr. Edgerton finished explaining what he planned to do, he asked if there were questions or observations in the audience.

A British doctor's voice asked, "Instead of trying to make an indentation under her lower lip, what about refracturing her jaws again and positioning them further back to give better symmetry?"

I tried to keep my face impassive, but my eyes widened with horror, as I remembered that dreadful surgery. Dr. Edgerton explained, "The jaws are in the best possible position, considering the amount of bone available. It will be much less traumatic to the patient to simply re-sculpt the tissue below the lips."

I relaxed the rigid tension holding my body. Dr. Edgerton had my best interests at heart; I did not have to worry.

Dr. Edgerton then asked, in his wonderful courteous way, "Would you like to say anything to the group, Gari?"

I stood up, reminded of how I enjoyed an audience despite my wearing a flapping hospital gown instead of a stylish dress for modeling. "Yes," I said, "I would like to thank all of you for the kindnesses you have shown me since I first came to UVA years ago. Most of you have gone out of your way to do thoughtful things for me when I least expected it. You understood that I needed to be reminded that I was not alone and that you were there to help me. I appreciate your compassion. I've laughed at all the timely jokes to keep my spirits up. And I appreciate the special help in teaching me to accept my face in transition as my own. I'm most grateful to Dr. Edgerton for the marvel of my new face. I thank him every morning when I look into the mirror. I hope you realize that you truly are miracle workers. I'm delighted with the way that you've changed my life and face in such a positive manner." I was surprised by the applause as I finished.

As I was whisked onto the stretcher down into the bowels of the hospital to the Operating Floor, I began listening to my "Pre-Op" tape again. I surrounded myself with calmness for the I.V. insertion and transfer onto the operating table. What a gift that the cold breezes, overly bright lights, loud noises, and unresisting table did not bother me as they had before! I positioned my tape player at the head of the table and changed to the "Inter-Op" tape. Dr. Persing began draping me with sterile cloths and washing my face with Betadine. I was afraid to try this complicated surgery with just the "Inter-Op" tape, so I had requested local shots of Xylocaine.

Dr. Edgerton entered and patted my shoulder. "You were terrific in the presentation, Gari. Thank you for the compliments. You must remember that you have a great deal to do with all this reconstructive healing, too."

I smiled. "You deserve every word I said and many more, Dr. Edgerton. I truly am grateful to you every time I look in the mirror."

He smiled back and said, "Thank you. Now for today, please keep your eyes closed and your face relaxed and immobile while we work. I'll make it as easy as possible for you. The nurse will make sure your tapes are running." I closed my eyes and smiled my last smile for a while. I concentrated on my peace-giving tapes and floated up onto my cloud of bliss.

It seemed as if only a fraction of a minute had passed when Dr. Edgerton patted me on the shoulder, saying, "We're finished for now, Gari. I know you wanted this to be the last, but I'd like to do a little more work in the future, if you agree. I'll have you taken to the Recovery Room and then back to your own room, when they feel you're ready."

I tried to open my eyes and smile at him and say thank you, but my face and eyes felt tightly bound into immobility. I relaxed back into the tapes. He would understand if I thanked him later. I was trans-ferred onto a stretcher and wheeled into the Recovery Room.

Forty-five minutes later, I was ready to go back to my room after I listened to only one side of the "Recovery" tape. I felt comforted to return to my room. I changed to the "Pain Control" tape. I could open a tiny slit of my eyelids by then but knew not to try to move my face. There were lovely flowers on my bedside table from Mum, and I noticed that I now had a roommate. The nurse explained that she was senile and might not react if I talked to her. I was not about to move my face to talk to anyone. I knew I had to remain as quiet as possible and listen to the tapes continuously to recover faster. I settled in to listen to the "Energy Walk," my favorite.

Later that evening, during doctor's rounds, I found out that the surgery (which I thought had been a fraction of a minute) had been five hours. My eyelids were red, swollen, and burned, but the cysts were gone. My cheeks had been pushed and pulled forward, more Z-shapes had been made in the straight lines on my chin, the indentation under my lower lip had been sculpted out, and my lips had been evened up. They felt sore when I touched them with my tongue. The lump had been removed from my foot and sent for analysis. Per usual, once Dr. Edgerton the artist had begun, he had found more and more to change to make me symmetrical and pretty. He did not want this surgery to be the last, despite my strong wishes. Though I felt uncomfortable and tired, I was grateful for his painstaking thoroughness. When Mum called, I reassured her that I was fine. Lee and Blair came by for short visits, bringing flowers. I was very glad to just rest with the tapes. I felt more tired and uncomfortable than I had expected.

About midnight, my roommate woke me up, yelling, "Ethel, get my shoes!" I turned on a tape and tried to go back to sleep. I had just relaxed again when she yelled out, "Ethel, get my shoes!"

"Ethel is not here," I mumbled, as I tried to concentrate on Robert Monroe's calm voice. After I lost count of the number of times she yelled, I rang for the nurse and explained what was going on. The nurse said that the lady slept all day, so she was alert at night. She explained to her that Ethel was not there and she did not need her shoes in bed. As soon as the nurse left, the yelling began again. After several hours, I gave up. I could not control the pain with the tapes unless I was uninterrupted, and I worried that I would not heal without sleep. I rang the nurse and asked for some codeine. I took the least possible dosage to enable me to sleep through the continued yelling, but the next day I felt drugged, dizzy, and weak. It made me realize that my body did not want to take drugs anymore. I was much better off with the tapes, if I had the privacy to use them. My roommate slept through the day peacefully although the nurses tried to wake her periodically. My I.V.s were taken out after doctor's rounds, and I tried to sleep with tapes as much as possible to make up for the night. Lee came by to ask if she could wash my hair again. We giggled as we remembered her washing it for me in the hospital kitchen years before.

That night, the same performance began. I called a nurse right away to ask if either I or my roommate could be moved to another room. There were none available; no one else would want to be with her. I was stuck. I turned up the volume as loud as possible and tried to relax and sleep. She yelled again and again. Finally, I gave up and asked for pain medicine. I was grateful that I would be going home the next day.

In the morning, the round of doctors decided that I looked good enough to travel. I quickly said goodbye and thank you to all of them, before they could change their minds. Tom and his father came to pick me up to drive to the airport. As we were leaving the hospital and I had to wait, on crutches, a long time for the elevator, I fainted. Luckily, they caught me before I fell. They propelled me out into the car, despite the hospital personnel wanting to examine and keep me. I did not want to return to Ethel's friend another night!

I enjoyed the drive to Dulles Airport through the rolling Virginia hills. They seemed tiny to me in comparison to the Colorado Rockies. When we arrived, the flight on my airline had been delayed due to snow in Denver. All I wanted was to get home to my own bed. Finally, our flight was called, and Tom pushed me in a wheelchair to the gate. Since my crutches were at home in Denver, I leaned on Tom's shoulder and hobbled onto the plane. We laughed together, as we remembered all the times I had leaned on him learning to walk. Two weeks on crutches would be a picnic compared to the past. The flight was smooth, and I felt better and better as the day wore on. I had called my friend Jane, who worked in Customer Service at my airline in Denver, and she had promised to meet our flight with a wheelchair and help me get off. A neighbor was to be at the airport to drive us home, but the concourses were very long and I still had no crutches. As the flight landed, Jane slipped in as soon as the door was open to tell me not to worry, that she had transportation for me. I felt privileged to belong to the inner circle of airline employees for special help when I needed it. I also gained an understanding of how grateful the handicapped are for assistance when traveling. Tom went out to find the neighbor who was driving us home. After the flight was empty, Jane maneuvered the airchair, which is the width to fit in airplane aisles, helped me transfer myself, then pushed me out. The cold bit my face as we went through the jetway. Remembering my accident, I felt fortunate to be inside from the cold stinging snow. What a contrast driving home in a Denver snowstorm was to the drive through the lovely green hills of Virginia that morning! I hoped the heat would warm the house quickly for us.

As we drove up our snow-filled driveway, I felt immense relief to be back in my own house away from Ethel's friend. Now I would be able to sleep and listen to my tapes in peace again. Tom bounded in the house and returned with my crutches from the cellar. I was afraid of falling in the snow, so he held onto me as we made our way up the stairs. We thanked the neighbor and patted Molly the cat, who was purring in ecstasy to see us. Peggy, the dog, was not at home, so Tom went next door and found her at the neighbor's, lying in her bed "looking like a queen." She always enjoyed our trips, as the neighbors gave her special attention. For the next two days, I tried to rest with the tapes as much as possible, to get stronger for work. The aftereffects of the codeine still seemed to drag me down; I realized that I would go to extra lengths in the future to avoid taking drugs.

As I hobbled on my crutches into my office on my first day back, I was unpleasantly surprised by the veiled looks of horror. I had forgotten how they stung my heart. I had been spoiled by a long time without surgery changing my appearance. I knew I must keep my courage up and stare back at the starers until they dropped their gazes in embarrassment. It was good to be distracted by the routine of my work, but I found I was exhausted by lunchtime. I asked the security department if there were any empty offices, where I could listen to my tapes at lunch. Luckily there was one with nice new carpeting, so I was able to lie on the floor and get a quick "tape fix" before eating lunch. I never could have made it through those days without the tapes.

When a week had passed, I was to have the stitches out. It began snowing that morning and I was afraid to drive, remembering my accident. Another employee noticed my worried manner and offered to deliver me back and forth. I learned to accept help gracefully. Finally, I could enjoy receiving without giving.

I was lucky at Frontier Airlines to have a new position in one of the office buildings away from the prying eyes of passengers. The transition to being scarred and ugly again was easier surrounded by a caring microcosm of fellow workers. They forgot to stare at me once they were past the first shock. I found I was glad to have urgent work to do; I was too busy to concentrate on my looks and worry about healing. At home, I found *AboutFace*, the book by Christine Piff which Dr. Edgerton's office had lent me, most inspiring to read. I kept thinking that if she had survived despite her face being ravaged by cancer, so could I after an accident. I joined the North American AboutFace organization and enjoyed their newsletters as a continuing help in my daily life to remember that I was not alone in facial disfigurement. They sent helpful information on insurance coverage and other aspects of looking unusual.

After the two weeks on crutches had passed, I rejoined yoga class. I relished doing some of the positions to feel stretched and released from the prison of my body. I had to think before starting any movement, however, about whether or not I would put my head below my heart and take care to adjust my body accordingly. If I forgot and lowered my head, my eyelids swelled and burned and throbbed. I wondered why any lady would want an eye lift by choice. I had to squat, instead of bending over, to make beds or reach anything in bottom drawers and cabinets. This was doubly hard for me due to my legs not being flexible from all the broken bones. The healing of my eyelids took a long time; instead of a magic day six months later when I could bend over again, there was a slow, gradual lessening of the throbbing for a few years. My eyelids never lost the purple tinge right by my lashes; people thought I always wore eye shadow.

Enough healing time had passed to begin speech therapy. This step proved to be just as much a challenge as all the other stages of laboriously relearning forgotten abilities. I was taught to do neck rolls to relax before I started. I augmented my chances of success by listening to a Monroe tape as well. I had to round my lips into a perfect circle as I watched in a mirror and said, "OOO-EEE." I had homework to tape each week—lists of words using sounds which I found difficult to pronounce. As I watched in the mirror, I was taught ways to even up my smile, pucker my lips, swallow correctly, and make a kissing noise. The most difficult of all to relearn was how to breathe out and laugh. I practiced humming up and down scales and tried to raise my voice in pitch so I could be heard more easily. Slowly I could hear progress on the homework tapes, but my voice would never regain the strength, range, or volume it had before because only one vocal cord worked properly. At least it was low and pleasing to the ear. My throat continued to be bothered by smoke, insecticides, and sharp smells, all of which immediately reduced my voice level.

Many changes happened over the next few years— Frontier Airlines was forced to declare bankruptcy, and I learned all about unemployment. Next, continuing to use my languages, I managed the Denver office of a fascinating international corporation which purified water with ozone. As all my scars settled in, people's reactions to my face were not as abrupt as before.

I found that they noticed my chin scars at first meeting but seemed to focus on my eyes after that first glance.

I kept up with my volunteer work, teaching the class about learning how to be single after divorce. I found that the newly single people in these classes were consumed with their own feelings of despair and never noticed how I looked. I taught how to answer and place personal ads and how to go out on a date, had a nurse lecture on the dangers of AIDS, and had the group discuss various relationship problems. My own concerns seemed minimal, as I listened to some of the disasters of others, while I slowly learned to become a single adult.

I enjoyed volunteering at the Denver Art Museum, which put me into the public eye and helped me over my fear of people's reactions to my face. The "Top of the Week" Jazz Party on Wednesdays rapidly became "The Singles' Event in Town"—it was more socially acceptable to say "I met so-and-so at the Museum" than at a bar. I loved the music and feeling of a fun party each week and slowly got to know more and more people.

I found I was most comfortable with personal ads for meeting appropriate men to date. The first ad I wrote had 100 answers. I interviewed them all on the phone first, to see if we had anything in common, before arranging a meeting for coffee or a glass of wine. Sometimes they would assume that I was beautiful from my low, seductive voice. I preferred having a chance to find out about them on the phone, without the immediate interference of my visual handicaps. I hated bars where no one could hear my soft voice and values were based on looks. I avoided meeting anyone for a meal, in case food dribbled down my chin, where I had no feeling. My selective dating made me feel as if I were back in college and popular again.

Tom continued with his sports and other interests. We saved time each week to do something special together, usually ending with a meal in his favorite restaurant, where he enjoyed reminding me to wipe my mouth. Emily visited us occasionally in Denver. While we had airline benefits, Tom, Emily, and I traveled around the United States and overseas. The children still acted as a buffer for me if people reacted to my appearance. It was interesting to me that more people stared at my face in my own country than in Europe or Third World countries, where disfigurement is a part of life. Each year the scars became fainter, needing less and less makeup to cover up. In fact, I seldom bothered using makeup anymore, feeling that people would either accept me as I was or not. I remembered Dr. Lambruschi telling me years ago that my chin scars were like a second smile. I had not found it amusing at all. Now that they had receded, I saw it as a secret second smile. I could accept my face, knowing I would never be perfect again; my priorities had changed in my new life. I tried to return my handicapped license plate, so as to feel normal, but the state of Colorado told me to keep it. I felt stigmatized by the mark, though admittedly there still were times when I was glad of the convenience of parking when my legs reacted to the barometer and refused to work for me.

In earlier stages of reconstruction, I had meandered along with surgeries, letting others dictate when and what happened to me. Now, it really was my choice whether to keep my face scarred or to undergo more refinement with all the changes and healing involved. If it were based on how I looked, I would not bother with any more surgeries. I no longer minded the road map of my life on my face. I knew what it was to be perfect looking and did not need that aspect of myself restored.

My life changed during 1989. Tom went away to school, my job ended due to relocation of the corporation, I sold my house, and I decided to let myself choose what I wanted. Before, I had always moved due to job openings or a husband's needs. For the first time, I could decide my future without putting others' needs in front of mine. The children would be home from college only for visits. I could forget needing to live in a good school district.

During that year, I took a creative writing class and was told to write about what I knew. For my first assignment, I wrote the beginning of this book. When I finished reading it out loud in class, I looked up to find the group sitting on the edges of their chairs with intent expressions on their faces.

One person broke the tension by asking, "What happens next, Gari?"

I smiled, happy that my writing had held their attention. The teacher interrupted. "Have you thought that this could be an excellent book if you draw it out?" With a flash of insight, I knew that this was to be my next career, the purpose of which my father had spoken during my near-death experience.

As a writer, I could live anywhere. Ironically, after deciding that I could go what I wanted, I had no idea what to choose. I found an old school map of the United States and began selecting. I eliminated all the northern states right away, as my bones were bothered by cold. I also did not want to live in the steamy south. I eliminated California due to congestion and being too far from Mum, in case she needed me. Arizona and New Mexico I loved, but the heat was intense in the summers. I wanted to be on the water, after leaving my beloved mountains. I settled on Florida, a few hours by air from Mum and the children's colleges. I read up on areas in Florida and flew there, driving around and looking over the countryside. It felt good to be making a change in my life for my own benefit. I decided on the west coast, which was less populated, packed up my things, put them in storage, went to Thailand with a friend for two months, returned, and moved, facing the fear of not knowing anyone in the area and not having a job to make it easier to meet people.

I found a sweet little house on the water, with a most spectacular view of the sunset. I was glad to be kind to myself and not just stay where fate had put me. The warm weather made my broken body limber. Instead of having to force myself to do my yoga and physical therapy despite the pain, I looked forward to feeling flexible, enjoying my mile-long walk and exercise each day. I remembered what I taught people in my Denver class—to follow their interests to make friends. I joined a ladies' sailing club and raced each week, relearning my skills from childhood. It was an easy way to have fun while I grew to know people of fascinating backgrounds, all with sailing in common. I also found a nearby yoga class, whose teacher introduced me to the Suncoast Yoga Teachers Association, where I could enjoy advanced yoga with similar souls. The yoga teacher became a cherished friend, who has thoughtfully helped me proofread every step of this book. I volunteered reading for the blind on WUSF, a local public radio station. I was assigned to read *The New Yorker* magazine and had fun describing the jokes on the air, as well as reading fascinating stories. When I applied for a license plate, I made no mention of needing a handicapped plate and received a regular number. What a thrill for me to have more proof of being real again!

When one is looking around the "people store" for friends, it is surprising how they appear right under one's nose. I met friends through church, while shopping, and even during doctors' visits. I searched the yellow pages until I found an optometrist with an ultrasonic cleaner for my contact lenses. Most eye doctors in Florida sent lenses out to be cleaned, with a week's wait, and I could not last that long with the pressure of glasses on my "rib nose." I was happy to find an office with the equipment necessary nearby. My appointment with this doctor was unlike any I had before. We barely discussed eyes, finding many other subjects in common; he was a true kindred spirit. I was fascinated and wanted to find out more about him. We began to develop a wonderful friendship, meeting for lunch periodically to compare our single lives and thoughts. I wondered what might come of this. This was typical of the way new friends entered my circle. I knew I was in the right place at the right time at long last.

Each Christmas, I sent Dr. Edgerton a card with a recent photo, so he could see how his work looked. He would usually write a thoughtful note back. I wondered if he made time in his busy schedule to do this for all his huge assortment of patients. Knowing the kind and gentle man that he was, I was sure he did. In 1989 I sent him a picture from Thailand of me standing in front of the Grand Palace in Bangkok. I was surprised when he wrote me, "It was great to get your note and the delightful photograph of you on your wonderful trip to the Far East. You look just great, and that wonderful smile warms my heart again...The facial symmetry seems excellent, and about the only thing that I see that might be considered for the future would be some minor work to blend out a few of the scars in the region of the chin and left lower cheek." At first, I felt I did not need any more surgery. Then I realized that he was an artist with an unfinished painting, and it was time. The details fell into place.

Chapter 16

The icing on the cake was my final surgery, in October 1990, which was filmed by The Monroe Institute while I used their Emergency Series tapes to control my pain. I doubted myself, as it had been five years since I had put my concentration and perseverance to the test. I kept feeling goldfish flickers of fear move around inside me, while I tried to remain strong. I flew to Charlottesville in stormy cold weather, with a bumpy instrument landing. Strangely, I never felt as nervous in a plane as I did in cars. I was concerned about keeping everyone waiting at the University of Virginia, since the flight was late. With my briefcase over my head, I ran through the torrents of rain to the terminal. I forgot how intense Virginia rain can be. My face lit up as I saw my friend Blair waiting inside.

"I thought you would like to be met, since the weather is bad," she said. "Why not cancel your rental car, and I will take you to the hospital? You have no need of a car after today."

As we hugged, I said, "How kind and thoughtful of you—you're just what I needed."

We drove to the University of Virginia, where we met Leslie France, the Professional Division Director of The Monroe Institute, and Patti LeMieux, who was to film my surgery. When the camera was set up, I gave a short interview, telling about my introduction to The Monroe Institute. Next they filmed Dr. Edgerton's assistant examining the scars on my chin. He reminded me that I could have a square graft from my abdomen to cover the entire chin, if I did not like the results of this revision. I responded, "I'm still not interested in a patch graft. I've seen photos. The edges are too apparent without a beard to hide them. This is the last surgery I ever want. Thank you for reminding me, though."

The four of us walked down the hall to Annette Selinger's office. She is the Nurse-Coordinator for the department and was to give us directions for our tour. I gave her a present I had brought for Dr. Edgerton, who was busy in emergency surgery. She promised to put it on his desk, where he would see it as soon as he returned. I pointed out the large bulletin board on her wall, filled with smiling photos of children, all of whose faces had been rebuilt by the department.

Annette remarked that, for her, the most interesting aspect of working under Dr. Edgerton was noticing how residents' attitudes and manners changed before and after rotations with Dr. Edgerton. Before their tour with him, most had little empathy for patients. Later, they acquired some of his gentlemanly compassion and courtliness, as they learned to deal with patients' feelings as well as bodies.

We walked over to the Virginia Ambulatory Surgery Center for our advance tour. I felt disassociated from the surroundings. I was used to being a patient in the hospital and seeing operating rooms in a nearsighted haze instead of sharp reality. The large carpeted waiting room was decorated in muted colors, with soft oversized upholstered chairs. I wondered if this was planned to accommodate the new overweight American. The ubiquitous television in a corner was mercifully silent. A separate tiled play area had toys, tables, and chairs. We next entered a preparation wing with dressing rooms, curtained cubicles with stretchers, and monitors for I.V. and blood pressure. The next section of the building was the operating wing, with large green swinging doors which opened by pressing rubber buttons in the hallways. The grey tiled operating room had recessed lights in the ceiling. In the center was the table lit by large adjustable ceiling lamps. Wheeled carts could be placed as needed around the table. From there, we entered an L-shaped wing for recovery, with a nurses' station in the center. Curtained cubicles for stretchers with monitoring equipment were in one end and adjustable padded red chairs were in the other. This last section circled back into the reception area.

Before Blair and I left the hospital for her house, I had blood drawn for tests and was photographed at several angles with different expressions on my face in black and white as well as color. We went to a lovely French restaurant for dinner that night, as we caught up on our lives. Old friends are especially harmonious in one's life, without the endless explanations required by a new one. I went to sleep calmly in the comfortable guest bed. I felt enveloped by the soft blue and rose floral sheets under a fluffy down quilt. My "Pre-Op" tape worked even more effectively in pleasant surroundings. I felt lucky to have Blair's house as a refuge, without the hospital hustle and bustle after surgery.

The next morning, Blair drove me to my reality at the hospital. We noticed the hazy speckled red and gold Blue Ridge Mountains, in contrast to the green pastures, as we drove past the large horse farms. The mist rose from the Rivanna River as we drove across and entered downtown Charlottesville. I felt at home with these memories and the familiar colonial brick buildings of Thomas Jefferson. I knew my surgery would go well.

Leslie and Patti met me with all their film equipment, as Blair dropped me off. I was given a name bracelet at the reception desk, then went to sit and concentrate on my tape in the waiting room. The tranquility with which Blair had enfolded me was in immediate danger from the blaring television cartoons within a circle of enraptured adults. Adding to the commotion, a baby was throwing noisy toys and crying in the play area, as his mother watched impassively. I despaired of finding my peace and solitude in this miasma of agitation. I sat as far from the noise as possible, turning up my volume full blast. I called on every shred of concentration in my being to block out the waiting room din. Thanks again to wonderful Robert Monroe's calm, reassuring voice, I succeeded.

I was startled away from my inner self by hearing my name called and opened my eyes to see Patti filming me. The nurse was ready for me in the preparation area. As I followed her, I felt grateful to be walking into surgery this time, instead of being pushed on a stretcher. My current well-being was invaluable to me now! I was told to remove all my clothing except my underpants and socks, then to put on the cotton gown, paper booties, and shower cap. In the hospital, no personal items are allowed. I felt an awareness of how much identity is related to possessions; hospitals rob one of selfhood. It is easier to heal as a person than as a non-person. My body felt cold in the dressing room, and I longed for some warm socks. My clothes were put into a large paper bag marked "CARTER"; that procedure gave me a feeling of finality, as though I was involved in a prison registration. I was now in the proper uniform for a lamb being readied for surgery.

I settled down on my stretcher, covered myself with two blankets against the cold, and turned on my tape player. I was interrupted several times by nurses, to gently insert an I.V. needle into my left hand, start up the electrolyte fluids, and monitor me. A large burly man was put into the curtained cubicle beside me. The nurse commented on his raised temperature and blood pressure, and his deep voice shook with nervousness as he asked what to expect. I felt a resurgence of gratefulness for the serenity of my Hemi-Sync tapes, as I remembered how terrified I used to be of anything dealing with surgery. I wished I could share my calm, but it was not the time.

Dr. Edgerton surprised me, as I concentrated on my tapes. He sat on the side of my stretcher and asked, "Good Morning, Gari. How are you?"

I smiled, appreciating his thoughtfulness, and answered, "Fine, thanks."

"I see you're working hard with your tapes again. Thank you for the pumpkin face you left on my desk last night. I had a long tiring day, and it gave me a good laugh just when I needed it."

"I'm so glad I could brighten your day a little. I feel I can never repay you for what you've done to create my face."

He smiled back at me. "Now, Gari, I understand that you don't want me to shave the lump off your nose, which I noticed the last time we saw each other. You only want me to do scar revision on your chin, right?"

"Yes, please, I responded. "I also wanted to ask you about two things. The grafted vermillion in my lips burns from sun exposure, as well as when I'm eating spicy food. Why is it super-sensitive?"

He looked through his bifocals at my lips. "Everyone's lips hurt from the sun, mine as well," he explained. "It's not the graft itself, but the fact that there are many more nerve endings under that skin now."

"So the answer is for me to live with it. Also, I'm drooling at times again. Is there anything you might do to help?"

"There are tight scars pulling your vermillion down on one side, which I could loosen when I am removing the largest lump of scar tissue," Dr. Edgerton offered.

"I would really appreciate not drooling. Thanks!"

"You'll be taken into the operating room after we both give interviews to the film crew. I'll see you shortly."

I smiled goodbye and slid into the security of my tapes.

When I was wheeled into an office for the next interview with the film crew, I told of my meeting with Dr. Edgerton the previous June, in which I asked permission for The Monroe Institute to film his surgery while I used the tapes again. He felt it could be arranged and wanted me on the fall surgery cancellation schedule. I repeated what I had said: "I really appreciate this, Dr. Edgerton. The tapes have helped me be calm, pain-free, and heal quickly, as you observed. I'd love the chance to help The Monroe Institute. They have never filmed a patient using their tapes before. Perhaps this can help pass on the gift of opening other people's eyes to being pain-free."

I told of visiting The Monroe Institute in Faber, south of Charlottesville, Virginia, during that trip. I was impressed with all the developments and progress since I had last been there. They now had a NRS-24 Neuromapper computer showing brain waves in a vibrant color-contour map to chart the difference between normal patterns and patterns during Hemi-Sync usage. Robert Monroe had written a second book and was finishing his third, and several biographies and technical books on Hemi-Sync had been published. A new series of tapes had been developed, called "H+" which stands for Human Plus. The tapes concentrate on teaching one how to balance, restore, and enhance all aspects of the body. The series ranges from heart improvement to appetite control to public speaking and restorative sleep. In addition, Hemi-Sync had been incorporated with music, to be used as a background while teaching autistic children and emotionally disturbed people, as well as entire school systems. Metamusic was developed to enhance creativity and to make one relaxed and free of stress. I tried several tapes, resolving to improve my eyesight among other goals. I found my favorite music to be "Midsummer Night," which begins with crickets and a gentle rain entwined with calm, relaxing music and tones. I was amazed at the leaps of advancement since my introduction to this world eight years before.

Next, I was wheeled down the hall. The nurse pushed a button on the wall, opening the green doors to the operating room. The room looked as it had the day before on the walk-through, though hazy without my contact lenses. Wonder of wonders, the table was padded and comfortable under my body, instead of the hard slab I remembered. There was even a pillow to put under my knees so that my back would not ache. I wound the earbud speakers behind my head and to the side, where the tape player would rest on a table. I was wrapped in soft blankets by the nurse, with one chilly foot poking out for a monitor point, and an automatic blood pressure cuff was put onto my arm above the I.V. needle. Then my arms were wrapped with sheets, with the ends tucked under my body. I remembered how terrified I was during the first few surgeries when I lost control of my tightly restrained arms. Now I knew to loosen the sheets a little by rolling my body and pulling my arms up, so they would not tense from immobility.

Dr. Edgerton's assistant entered and began to sterilize my face, using cold, wet, orange Betadine sponges. He draped sterile sheets all over my face and head, as if creating a medieval wimple. It was harder and harder to keep my concentration on the tapes with all the noisy commotion. I took a deep yogic cleansing breath and tried to relax back into Robert Monroe's voice telling me how everyone was working to help me. Suddenly I heard his voice in my left ear speaker instead of always the right side. I smiled at the film crew, saying that I had forgotten this change in the tape used during surgery.

Dr. Edgerton entered the Operating Room, greeted me, and began explaining my face and its problems to his assistant. He wanted to remove four intersecting scars which formed a raised square on my chin. He asked me to smile so that he could follow the changes in my second smile line, which still ran in a semi-circle shape from ear to ear. As they finished analyzing how to best achieve a smooth chin for me, he said, "Now please relax your jaw, Gari. I need it to be as loose and floppy as possible for my work."

I forced myself to relax my body, but I felt an uncontrollable butterfly of tension emerge in my solar plexus. Suddenly, I doubted my stamina and concentration abilities. I realized that I needed more help. I did not want to break down in front of the camera and ruin the film for The Monroe Institute after all the help they had given me. I asked, "Could I please have something to take off the edge?" I did not say, "edge of terror," but meant it. Dr. Edgerton ordered a small dose of Demerol to be added to my I.V. solution. I realized that I deserved the extra sedation, as Dr. Edgerton's surgeries were legendary in length due to his meticulous art. I felt myself flying down the sliding board of oblivion with the Demerol, and I concentrated on my tape as the tension flew up and out of me.

In the Operating Room, I feel totally disassociated from my body as if I were on the ceiling, dispassionately observing what the surgeons are doing. My body registers pricks from Xylocaine and the pushing of cutting and stitching without a care or reaction, while my spirit floats in happiness. I can liken it only to the exhilaration of skiing, when I feel as if I were flying, or sailing when the wind is just right and I skim the water. I always experience great resistance leaving that state of perfect bliss.

Suddenly, Dr. Edgerton's voice interrupted Robert Monroe's on my tape. "Gari, I read your manuscript last night."

I pushed my voice through the web of calm, careful to talk without moving my jaw. "Dr. Edgerton, I'm sorry, but it's hard for me to hear you as well as concentrate on the Hemi-Sync tapes."

I could hear him smile at me as he said, "Perhaps this isn't the best time to discuss your book. We'll do it later."

I slid back into my cloud, wondering if there would be a time but not caring right then. It was more important for me to relax for the surgery at that moment. The nurse flipped my tape each time it ended, so I had continuous sound. After two hours of surgery, Dr. Edgerton said he was late for rounds and dashed off. His resident closed the last incisions, removed my sterile wimple, and fashioned a bulky bandage on my chin. I kept my tape going as I talked to him. He wrote me a prescription for Keflex, to combat infection, and asked if I wanted any pain medication.

"No thanks, the tapes are all I need," I mumbled through my lips. He looked surprised, and I wondered if I sounded drunk. I felt perfectly alert.

Patti continued filming, as the nurses helped me move from the operating table onto the stretcher. I clutched my tape player, anxious to change the "Intra-Op" tape for the "Recovery" one. My body dissolved into tiredness, though my mind was alert. I was wheeled into the Recovery Room with my head raised for the camera. My mouth was full of cottony dryness, and I was given a glass of water to drink before my next interview. I was grateful for the precious cool relief rushing down my throat before I had to speak. They asked me if I remembered requesting my tapes to be flipped during surgery.

"I most definitely remember," I answered. "When the tape ends, one plummets to reality from that fluffy cloud of serenity. I felt like an addict needing a fix because I wanted that tape back on urgently without delay. When I listen to the tapes, I float above all the surgical action and am aware of what's going on from a remote perspective." I explained my feelings for a few more minutes, as fatigue gushed into the lake of my being. I was grateful when the camera stopped, as I needed to be flat, listening to the "Recovery" tape. I floated on my tape-induced cloud of peace, which dissolved partially and then re-formed as the nurses checked on my blood pressure. I did not want the peaceful journey of recovery to end.

After several hours, a nurse wheeled me to a chair, removed my I.V. needle, and gave me apple juice to drink. I dressed and walked out with the nurse to meet Blair, who had her car waiting for me. As I climbed inside, I realized that I would be tapeless and insecure during the drive to her house, and I felt an addict's panic rise in my throat. *I must remember what I had done before and empower myself to survive again*, I thought. If I had gone this far with the final surgery, I could and would continue. The drive was calmly painfree as we chatted. I called Mum to reassure her after we arrived and snuggled in bed with my "Pain Control" tape to return to the peaceful center of my being.

I awoke to the delicious aroma of potato leek soup slipping under my door. Blair had made a huge pot, thinking of my difficulties eating with a bandaged jaw. Tears pricked my eyes as I remembered all she had done for me over the years—keeping my children the night of the accident, taking me on my first outing to the movies, giving multitudes of visits and presents. Remembering my love of chocolate, she thoughtfully had a rich orange-chocolate cake for dessert, as my reward to celebrate my last surgery. After a delicious family dinner together, I slept well with my tapes. The next day I lazily healed, napping and talking, enfolded by my good friends. Lee picked me up the next morning for brunch and marathon talking, before driving me to the airport.

When I was in line at the airport, I noticed Dr. Persing from UVA ahead of me. I smiled and said, "Dr. Persing, I'm not sure if you remember me from many years ago. I'm Gari Carter. You worked on my nose and face during your residency."

"Of course I remember you, Gari. How are you? What did 'Dr. E' do to your face this time?"

Our conversation was interrupted to board the flight, but we managed to sit together to catch up. I was struck by the change in him from a hesitant resident to a smooth, courtly gentleman like Dr. Edgerton. He had become Chief of the Craniofacial Clinic and sponsored a trip to India to do volunteer surgery on Third World children each year. He encountered amazingly primitive conditions as well as horrendous defects. He said that the gratitude of patients was the same the world over. He recalled a discussion about me years ago when a slide of my face was on the screen in the auditorium.

A residents asked, "How do you have the courage to cut into the face of a beautiful woman? What if you make it worse?" He said that this universal fear of new doctors makes many slow-handed in the operating room, until they gain confidence.

Hearing this, I was filled with gratitude again for Dr. Edgerton's magical Michelangelo-like skill creating my face while teaching. Dr. Persing was pleased at the changes in my face as he peeked under the bandages to see the latest corrections. We both said how glad we were that the other's life had evolved happily, as the flight ended and we parted.

Epilogue

I was glad to be home in my own little bed in sunny Florida. The warm weather enhanced my healing after surgery, though the tiredness slowed me down. Whenever I felt twinges of sadness from exhaustion, I remembered my lesson from the ugly green chair in the hospital years ago. This, with all I learned in the meantime, gave me courage to recover rapidly from this surgery. Dr. Chuong, who had made my jaw years ago, had also moved to Florida. He kindly removed my stitches ten days later, and his hands were as gentle as I remembered. He was glad to see that his work had healed well and that my bite was still perfect. I began having Neuromuscular Therapy to reduce the scar tissue buildup in my chin, as well as Craniosacral Therapy to re-balance my head and spine. Though I continued using Monroe tapes, I found I had less need of pain control than before. Now I had the extra backup of the "H+" Series and enjoyed "Regenerate," "Restorative Sleep," "Emergency-Injury," "Circulation," and "Tune-up" regularly. I felt strengthened by an abundance of healing help from which to choose. My eyesight kept improving from the vision tape. The new scars receded rapidly. All redness and puffiness was gone within a month.

When I began to write this book, I cried. My body hurt with intense physical horror, in whichever spot about which I wrote. I wanted to stop and forget it all. My father had told me that I had something else to accomplish in my lifetime, during my near-death experience. I did not know what he meant until I began writing this and subsequent books. I had searched in vain for mentors and heroes in my voyage of reconstruction. Now, my experiences could help others.

In re-reading the first draft, I noticed where I distanced myself in writing about certain events. It was just like the stages of illness—doubt and denial, anger, acceptance, and peace. All I could deal with at first were the facts. I hid from the true anguish and hurt. Later, I found it healing to write the final layer of emotion into this segment of my life. Since time had no meaning to me in the time period immediately after the accident, there deliberately are not many references to time.

With one exception, my family and friends chose their own pseudonyms for this book. The names of the doctors and The Monroe Institute personnel are their own. My mother is happily back home. Tom is a six-and-a-half-foot-tall college student in South Carolina. Emily graduated from college and is contentedly teaching in Virginia. My broken bones and I adore living in Florida's balmy climate.

My sweeping journey from independence to dependence and back filled almost ten years of my life. I now realize that my new expanded life was entwined with giving and receiving openly with those surrounding me. My life has been enriched by all those who helped me on my way to recovery. At first, I longed for a mentor to sponsor me in my battle to come back after my tragedy. Since I never found my hero, I became my own, as I managed alone. I learned how to transform my trauma into an enjoyable challenge. I worked on mastering my goal to become a person of integrity, courage, resilience, and perseverance. My self-image was balanced instead of being based on outward appearances, as it was in my first life. I realize that, in all our lives, we either experience or have someone we love go through difficult times in one way or another. The perception, rather than the actual incident, is of crucial importance to one's well-being. My tragedy evolved from the worst to the best event in my life. My recovery shows that the mind, body, and soul can be transformed. I did it—You can also!

Appendix

A listing of craniofacial centers in this country and throughout the world may be obtained by writing directly to the International Society of Craniofacial Surgery, 130 Rue de la Pompe, 75116 Paris, France. They can provide information for specific localities.

For those readers interested in the AboutFace organization, their U.S. address is: Pamela Onyx, Director, AboutFace USA, P.O. Box 737, Warrington, PA 18976 (1-800-225-FACE). The Canadian branch publishes the newsletter: AboutFace, 99 Crowns Lane, 3rd floor, Toronto, Ontario, Canada M5R 3P4 (416-944-FACE).

The following article from *TMI FOCUS*, Vol XII, No. 4, Fall 1990, entitled, "What is Hemi-Sync?" by Leslie France, Director, Professional Division of The Monroe Institute, explains the technical side of the Monroe Institute's tapes which I used during my surgeries. For further information on the tapes or the film of my surgery, please contact: The Monroe Institute, Route 1, Box 175, Faber, VA 22938. Their phone number is (804) 361-1252. The commercial arm which handles orders of tapes is: Interstate Industries., Inc., P.O. Box 505, Lovingston, VA 22949. Their phone numbers are (804) 263-8692, (800) 541-2488 for credit card orders, and (804) 263-8699 FAX.

What Is Hemi-Sync?

by Leslie France
Director, Professional Division
The Monroe Institute

In response to this question, The Monroe Institute has published quantities of explanatory literature over the years. By now, most people with a lively curiosity about mind-brain technology know that:

1. Hemi-Sync is a noninvasive technology based on two fundamental, naturally occurring auditory phenomena: frequency following response (FFR) and binaural beat stimulation.

2. FFR is essentially a process of entrainment whereby, when a listener's audio environment is dominated by sounds of specific frequencies, the listener tends to reproduce those frequencies within his/her own physiology. Further, the listener can become entrained to the state of awareness engendered by those frequencies. Over time, individuals can learn to reproduce the state at will without continuous external audio stimulation.

3. Binaural ("two-ears") beats are produced within the physiology of a listener when different audio frequencies are introduced into each ear. The brain-mind discerns this difference and strives to bridge the gap. It therefore produces a third frequency, which is the difference between the two, and which is not an actual sound but may be perceived as an oscillating sound. To cite the usual example: if 100 Hz (cycles per second) is introduced into the left ear, and 104 Hz is introduced into the right, the binaural beat frequency will be 4 Hz.

4. The beauty of a binaural beat system is that: (a) it provides the opportunity for a listener to be influenced by frequencies below the threshold of normal human hearing (we generally have trouble hearing sounds below 40 Hz), and (b) it tends to stimulate a state of low-frequency brain-wave interhemispheric synchronization. The results of such synchrony include an amplification in the attention a listener is able to apply while in this state. Although interhemispheric synchronization occurs naturally, it is usually intermittent and of limited duration. Binaural beat stimulation aids the listener to sustain it, thereby greatly increasing one's ability to maintain a unique focus of attention over relatively long periods of time.

5. The sounds which are used to stimulate binaural beats (in the example above, the 100 Hz and 104 Hz frequencies) are called "carrier frequencies."

6. The Monroe Institute works with beat frequencies primarily in the Beta, Alpha, Theta, and Delta ranges.

Add to these basics the fact that certain frequency combinations have been identified as conducive to stimulating various, specific mind-brain states.

To review, this process quickly guides an individual into a targeted, sustained state of awareness, within which s/he is able to apply a unique focus of attention toward achieving his/her desired outcome. Furthermore, s/he learns to reproduce the state at will.

This, then, is the common knowledge—the body of technical components which support the spirit of the Hemi-Sync systems. Entrainment to sound frequencies and binaural beat stimulation are neither patented nor copyrighted by The Monroe Institute. They occur naturally and spontaneously; they were not invented, but rather harnessed and directed by the Institute.

Perhaps an appropriate question to pose at this juncture is: *what is not Hemi-Sync?* Due to the burgeoning interest in current brain-mind technology over the last decade or so, including a proliferation of hardware, a list of what is not Hemi-Sync would fill a small telephone book. Suffice it to say, only those systems designated with one or more of the Institute's registered trademarks are Hemi-Sync. Any programs, tapes, hardware, or software bearing a registered Hemi-Sync trademark or trade name of The Monroe Institute or Interstate Industries, Inc., without authorization of The Monroe Institute or Interstate Industries, Inc., are in violation of copyright law.

The importance of making this distinction far exceeds any legal implications. You need to know that, when you choose to utilize Hemi-Sync, you are taking advantage of more than a quarter-century of research and development that have brought The Monroe Institute's sound technology to its present level of evolution. Inherent in this advantage is the spirit of Hemi-Sync — *the precisely identified, controlled, and proven complex frequency combinations themselves.*

Within the carrier and beat frequency ranges out of which Hemi-Sync signals are selected are a virtually limitless sea of individual frequencies from which to choose. Through meticulous, provocative, and sometimes boring research and trial and error at the Institute laboratory, specific combinations were discovered to elicit certain results: some beneficial, some ineffective, and others that were found to be potentially harmful. Beneficial frequency combinations were refined further and integrated into larger systems. These became Hemi-Sync frequencies. Ineffective patterns were discarded, and potentially harmful signals were noted as such and avoided. This process of identification, classification, and evaluation continues today.

The process, while ultimately resulting in the compilation of a vast inventory of highly effective signal patterns, is analogous to emptying the sea with a bucket. The nature of the water remaining in the sea is anybody's guess. Some will eventually become a part of the Hemi-Sync inventory. Many will not pass the Institute's evaluation standards.

Since the late 1950s we have been accumulating

the body of knowledge which allows us to configure sound wave forms accurately into the subtle and powerful consciousness tools you are using. Following the frequency evaluation, the architecture of the Hemi-Sync sound patterns is designed. The relationships between the beat and carrier frequencies are identified and fine-tuned: the number, positions, and amplitudes of the superimposed frequencies are determined. Finally, the flow of merging and separation of these complex combinations is established depending upon the purpose of a particular exercise. All of these contributing details eventually culminate in a Hemi-Sync tape.

Herein lies the essence of what Hemi-Sync is and is not. Hemi-Sync is: complex combinations of sound frequencies which have been found to be beneficial and which are subsequently utilized within Hemi-Sync systems designed and produced by The Monroe Institute. Hemi-Sync is not: any combination of binaural beat and carrier frequencies, either purposefully or randomly selected, by other than The Monroe Institute.

We offer this information to clarify the Institute's position within the growing industry of brain-mind research and technology. Throughout the past twenty-five years we have witnessed the cultural perception of this arena change from considering such research as occult-inspired phenomenology to the wave of the future. We are proud to be one of the pioneers in this field. And, we are pleased to share this valuable work with the many others who are attracted by its potential.

Photo by Barry Croombs

Gari Carter was born in Baltimore and grew up in Maryland and Connecticut. She studied at Randolph-Macon Woman's College, Middlebury College, and the University of Virginia. She lives on the west coast of Florida.